ARCHITECTURE ASIA

arcasia
Architects Regional Council Asia

中國建築學會 The Architectural Society of China

Journal of the Architects Regional Council Asia (ARCAS

Co-Publishers

The Architectural Society of China (ASC)
9 Sanlihe Road, Beijing, China, 100835

Tongji University
1239 Siping Road, Shanghai, China, 200092

Sponsor

Tongji Architectural Design (Group) Co., Ltd.
1230 Siping Road, Shanghai, China, 200092

Contents

Editorial

Apurva BOSE DUTTA, Author, Architectural journalist, Curator, Editor, and Educator

Guest Editor
Website: www.apurvabose.com
Email: apurvabose@yahoo.com
LinkedIn, Instagram handles:
@apurvabosedutta

Apurva Bose Dutta is an Indian author, award-winning architectural journalist, curator, editor, and educator based in Bengaluru, India. An alumna of the Chandigarh College of Architecture (2005), Apurva has taken a professional journey of 19 years that has seen global collaborations with architecture-design multimedia publication houses, firms, organizations, and institutions. Apurva works at the intersection of architectural design writing, curation, critique, discourse, communications, and thinking. She is passionate about writing, curating architecture-design content and discourses, and professional speaking, offers training initiatives in architectural writing, and consults for academic and professional platforms. Recognized for her pioneering work in architecture design writing and focussing on increasing the subject's visibility in India, Apurva has been invited by the Australian and Finnish governments to represent the Indian delegation of architectural writers as part of international media visits to Melbourne (2016) and Helsinki (2018). Author of *Architectural Inheritance and Evolution in India* (2023) and *Architectural Voices of India* (2017), Apurva is widely published and holds advisory positions with several renowned global architectural and design platforms.

Spaces and *emotions* are fundamentally connected. The impact of built spaces on human emotions has been realized over time; this special issue of *Architecture Asia* extends its consideration to an additional "typology" of space: that offered by the written word. *Spaces*, *words*, and *emotions* sit contentedly at the ends of a triangle, holding on to their distinctiveness while coexisting as a trio, complementing, affecting, and engaging with each other. The multiplicity of these three entities in terms of internal and external articulations with their constant transformations generates the premise for life to exist. This curated issue offers a window to the perspectives of and approaches to literary and built spaces and, consequently, their most absolute and intangible consequence: the *emotion* they elicit.

Written accounts by invited architects and academics attest to the mutual bond of writing, literature, and architecture, and how they influence and transform each other: the architectural structure camouflaged in writing, and writing serving additional forms of notation for built/unbuilt spaces while assuming the core of theory, history, and criticism. Presenting global perspectives and the history of writing and its evolution in the industry and mainstream media, the essays depict that writing and literature are foundational to architecture, and their lack leads to diminished knowledge, perception, and recognition of the latter. Considering the power of present-day's digital media, this introspection broadens the potential of writing and critiquing the built environment to every being, making them more responsive to their built world. A call for action is made—a "literary emergency" urging intellectual and critical writing that harbors a sense of "abstraction" and which can catalyze discourses relevant to the built environment.

Alongside, a curated collection of architecture and urban design projects across Asia adds to this literature and vocabulary. One could read these design interventions as literary texts to deduce how they, individualistic in their geography, typology, function, spatial exploration, articulation, and user profile, imbibe the core tenets of representing and safeguarding their nation's culture and heritage. Effectively responding to their client's and context's requirements, a common prevailing denominator underscores the designs' intention to engage with their users ardently.

The sparsely illustrated essays and abundantly illustrated projects assert the relevance of different mediums to communicate the art and science of building. It is time to decipher how to retain the balance between these diverse mediums of communication to comprehend, impact, and revolutionize the built environment efficiently.

Writing Habitation and Inhabiting Writing

Prem CHANDAVARKAR, CnT Architects

Prem Chandavarkar is the managing partner of CnT Architects, an award-winning and widely published architectural practice based in Bengaluru, India. He received his training from the School of Planning & Architecture, New Delhi (B. Arch. 1978), and the University of Oregon, USA (M.Arch. 1982). He is a former Executive Director of Srishti Manipal Institute of Art Design & Technology in Bengaluru and is an academic advisor and guest faculty at Indian and international colleges of architecture. Besides his design practice at CnT, he writes, lectures, and blogs on architecture, urbanism, philosophy, politics, education, environment, art, and cultural studies.

Abstract

Writing is typically seen as a core component of architecture's ability to reflect on itself. But the relationship between writing and architecture is nuanced and complex, sometimes competitive, and the history of the relationship has even led to pitfalls of abstraction and distraction. This essay examines this history, the complications it has unleashed, and suggests that we should understand the nature of reflective practice, and architecture's experiential roots. Further, rather than looking at writing too directly, we should seek an indirect literary lens that reveals how translation and poetry are modes of being and design practice.

Author Information
Prem CHANDAVARKAR: prem.cnt@gmail.com

Keywords

Architecture, writing, abstraction, reflective practice, translation, metaphor.

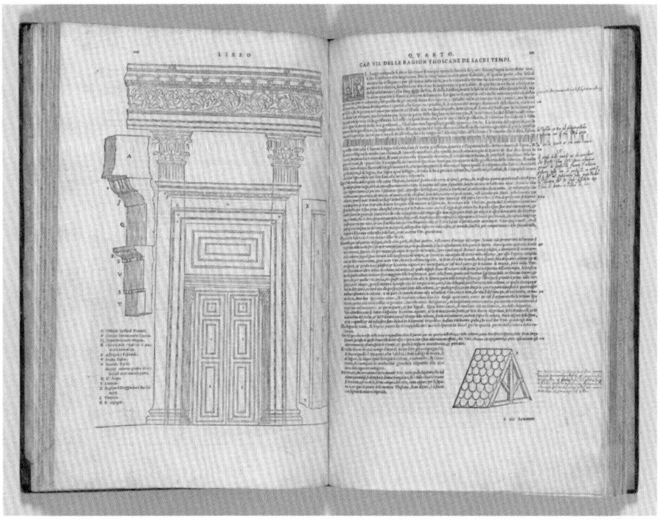

Figure 1
Inner pages of *Ten Books on Architecture* by Marcus Vitruvius Pollio

Figure 2
New Inventions of Modern Times [Nova Reperta], *The Invention of Book Printing*, plate 4

1. Introduction: What Does Writing Do for the Modern Profession of Architecture?

While the products of architectural design are tectonic and spatial rather than literary or verbal, there is little doubt that writing lies at the heart of the discipline. Based on that theory, criticism and the history of architecture cannot exist without writing, so it is easy to assume that writing underpins a reflective dimension of the profession without which architecture would be hard-pressed to sustain or expand its creative vision. But is the relationship between writing and architecture truly so close and foundational? Or is it more nuanced and complex? Is writing both facilitative and obstructive to architecture? This essay seeks to tackle these questions, to throw some light on the relationship between writing and architecture and ask how it may determine the future of architecture. To do so, it will confine itself to the history of how writing is consumed within the profession to shape architectural practice; architectural journalism directed toward the public will not be covered.

Written treatises on architecture have existed since the dawn of civilization (Figure 1), but many of these early treatises precede the birth of architecture as a specialist profession separated from the anonymous tradition of master-builders. The profession, as we know it today, consisting of named individuals who specialize in architecture as a design discipline standing apart from construction, came about only in the late fifteenth century in Europe during the Renaissance period.

If our interest is in the contemporary relationship between writing and architecture, then analysis must go past these early treatises and begin with two transformational developments that are foundational to modern practice. First, is the metamorphosis of writing itself, through the invention of the printing press in the mid-fifteenth century and the development of a book publishing industry that emerged by the late fifteenth century, followed by newspaper publishing in the early seventeenth century and magazine publishing by the late seventeenth century. Second, is the emergence of architecture as a distinct professional discipline constituted by individuals who have undergone specialized professional training in the field within institutions created for that specific purpose, beginning with the establishment of the École Nationale Supérieure des Beaux-Arts de Paris (Ecole des Beaux-Arts de Paris), France, in the mid-seventeenth century.

2. Printing and Architecture's Fall in Status

The invention of printing was a transformational event that led to writing having a foundational and disruptive impact on architecture (Figure 2). This was first highlighted by Victor Hugo in his novel *The Hunchback of Notre-Dame*, in a scene set in the deaconry of Notre-Dame (Paris, France), where the deacon, Don Claude Frollo, gestures to a book on his desk and an adjacent window that frames a view of the cathedral and remarks, "Alas, the one will kill the other ... the book will kill the building."[1] Hugo goes on, in an entire chapter devoted to the subject of architecture, to expound on this enigmatic declaration.[2] Every generation holds foundational values it believes to be eternal, and consequently seeks a medium in which it can immortalize these values to pass them on to future generations. Until the advent of printing, architecture was the most stable medium for this immortalization of value, and its spatial

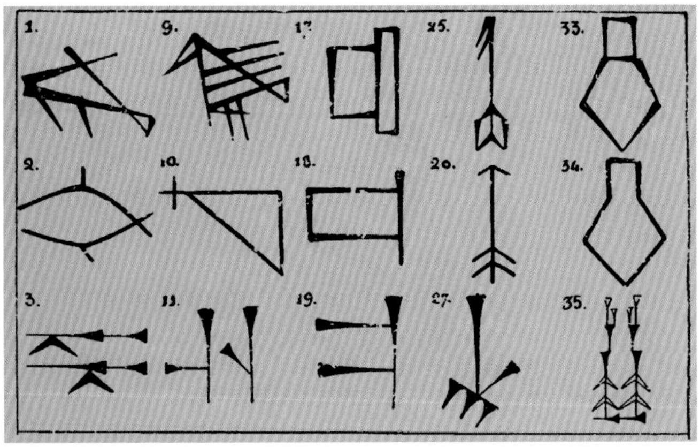

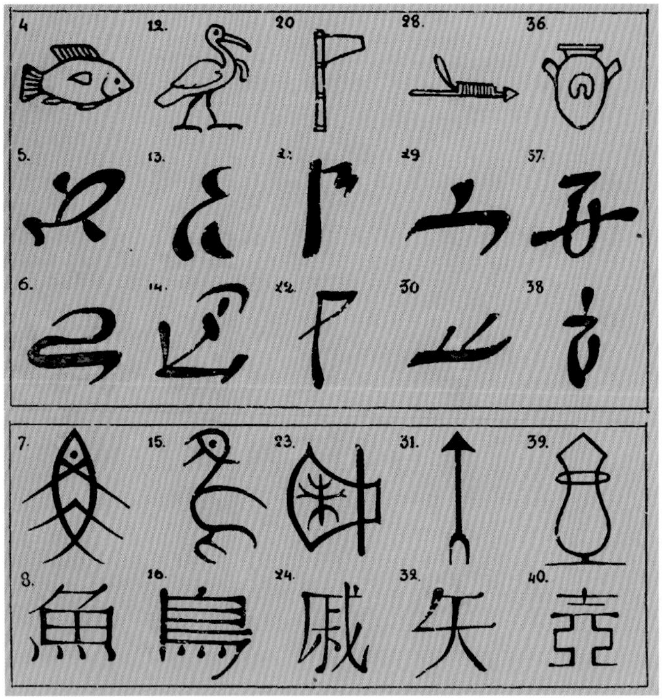

Figure 3
Cuneiform, Egyptian, and Chinese writings at different times by various processes

arrangements, narratives of ornament, symbolism of proportion, and rituals consecrated within it, all served to make architecture a living register of humanity's dreams, ideals, and myths. This changed with printing. Now, an idea could be reproduced thousands of times to spread over vast geographies. Architecture could not combat this ubiquity. The printed word replaced architecture as the register of human thought and architecture lost its historic status as the "mother of the arts." Recognizing a fall from foundational symbolism to utilitarian purpose, Hugo wrote, "The beautiful lines of art give way to the cold and inexorable lines of geometry. A building ceases to be a building; it is a polyhedron."[3]

3. The Impact of Notation

One must remember that writing is a form of notation (Figure 3), and with professional training beginning in the Ecole des Beaux-Arts de Paris, another form of notation became foundational to architectural thought and practice: the use of drawings to represent architectural designs and ideas. Until then, architecture was primarily conceptualized through rudimentary sketches that formed the launching pad for subsequent improvization within the construction process. Ecole des Beaux-Arts de Paris, attempting professional education as a specialized activity for the first time, needed a code that allowed architectural discourse to flourish purely within the academic institution, and so launched the idea of drawing as a rigorous form of notation that allowed imagining architecture as an abstract process detached from the construction site. Over time, this became institutionalized across the profession as a dominant means of architectural thought. According to Alan Colquhoun,[4] this had two significant impacts: drawing became a code through which architectural thought could be contemplated for consequent abstract reflection, and it led to a division of labor between the one who composes architecture at a desk and the one who interprets the composition to execute it at site. These two developments led to an exponential rise in the intensity with which architecture could be imagined. The notational code acted as a visual aid to memory and contemplation, and the division of labor granted sheltered time for reflection outside the exigencies of construction. Ecole des Beaux-Arts de Paris led to the flowering of the theory of architecture to a level that had never been seen before. This impact that notation had on architecture is affirmed by a similar development in another art that took place around the same time as the early years of establishment of Ecole des Beaux-Arts de Paris: music's widespread adoption of modern staff notation, based on a system of five lines and four spaces, that allowed, for the first time, the notation of a composition in terms of pitch, melody, and rhythm. This led to the emergence of complex compositional forms such as the symphony, which had not been possible with earlier primitive forms of notation that were not as comprehensive.

These developments allowed theory to flourish as an activity in its own right: an academic activity that could be institutionalized in a space segregated from design practice. Writing on architecture became integrated into the culture of the profession; theory became both a practice and a subject of study within architectural academia; and architectural journalism came into being, first as columns on architecture within general magazines in the eighteenth century, and eventually specialized journals on architecture by the nineteenth century.

In these early years of establishing a professional culture of architectural practice and academia, theory was shaped by a belief established in Europe during the Protestant Reformation—that one had to discern and reject the negative effects of civilization to go back to humanity's original state of happiness. Early inhabitation of nature, with the Garden of Eden as a prevailing metaphor, was seen as a call to return to sacred origins uncontaminated by the corrupting influence of civilization; a philosophy that came to be known as the myth of the noble savage. The primitive hut of those times was seen as inspiration and led to two primary schools of architectural thought: a neoclassical school that saw the pediment as representing this hut, and a neo-Gothic school that saw the style's organic hierarchies as more representative of the state of nature.

Writing and drawing, as forms of notation, radically reshaped the profession. One could ask whether there is a general principle of notation involved that manifests in both modes. Or, do the peculiarities of each of these forms have distinctive effects? But first, it is necessary to recognize that it is not just the introduction of these notational systems that was significant, but also their ubiquity.

4. Literacy and Abstraction

As Walter J. Ong has shown, language was transformed by the technology of printing, to cause a shift of the linguistic foundations of society from orality to literacy.[5] Oral cultures could not depend on the widespread dissemination of written texts as mnemonic aids to cultural memory. A reliance on oral language tends toward the use of repetitive linguistic rhythms that facilitate remembering; a great deal of cultural memory is held in songs and verse kept alive through repetitious and participatory retelling. Being founded on memory, the governance of oral cultures tends to be conservative—not necessarily in the sense that it is understood in politics today, but in a cyclical sense of time that ritualizes retelling, to sustain a rhythmic return to sacred origins. On the other hand, literacy—especially once it becomes sufficiently widespread—allows a degree of abstraction because it is now detached from embodied participation. The mere presence and reliability of texts as repositories of cultural memory allows the delegation of the act of remembering to preserve cultural memory, even if these texts are rarely read. Texts change from an emphasis on rhythm to the development of linear narrative. Abstraction allows the imagination of conditions never seen, and with the contemporaneous advent of democratic politics, the sense of time changes, from a cyclical rhythm to a linear trajectory aimed at a better future.

A similar increase in abstraction occurred in architectural thought. Drawing not only fostered architectural thought, but also expanded to underpin the entire process of producing architecture, with the emergence of practices in the late eighteenth century—such as the Adam Brothers,[6] who set the precedent for what would become the dominant form of practice: a detailed and holistic documentation of design in drawings made prior to construction, reducing the scope for crafted tectonic creativity on-site. Reflection became the province of architectural practice, with the site reduced to mere techniques of implementation. With the spread of a capitalist industrial economy, demands rose for new public typologies, such as railway stations, large office buildings, airports, and hotels, that were not anchored in social and moral purpose in the way that institutions in pre-capitalist societies imparted significance to the public realm. The earlier classical notion that Ecole des Beaux-Arts de Paris sought to take over—that an eternal and pervasive divine field must be humanized and ordered within each project—gives way to an abstracted perception of "a heterotopic space which consists of individual buildings unrelated—both conceptually and phenomenally—to their neighbors."[7]

A second major turn of theory supported these developments. By the early twentieth century, the earlier notion of always seeking a return to sacred origins had given way to sights cast on the future rather than the past. Traditional styles were seen as repressive and unaccommodating to the new urban forms; building types and technologies unleashed by the Industrial Revolution brought about developments that represented a hope of unshackling humanity into new freedoms. The machine displaced the primitive hut to become the prevailing metaphor, and the well-known dictum "form follows function" came to suggest a functional and technological aesthetic representing a liberatory social and historical purpose. In the international aesthetics of abstraction that ensued, architects leveraged this style, claiming it to be best suited to deliver the promise of technological innovation that would change society for the better. A great deal of writing during this period adopted teleological utopian goals and was highly rhetorical in style to convey a revolutionary fervor in which the architect was cast as a missionary leader to humanity. The Staatliches Bauhaus (Bauhaus), Germany, replaced Ecole des Beaux-Arts de Paris as the prototypical architectural academy.

But by the last quarter of the twentieth century, once the abstracted expression of technical rationality was no longer novel, this zeal had run out of steam. Modern architecture become an aesthetic rather than ethical project, where designs seemed to align more with capitalism than with social revolution, and the revolutionary enthusiasm of the architect was rejected as being a mask for megalomania.

As a means of critical renewal, what could writing offer to such a situation? How could architecture recover cultural significance? A classicist reliance on eternal truth handed to us by tradition had been rejected as having no place in a world of economic and technological innovation. The liberating future that early twentieth century modernism had anticipated appeared to be stillborn. Some recovery was sought in a turn to the social sciences and we saw writing that suggested that meaning could be recovered through anthropological analysis,[8] but no adequate resolution was found on how to absorb this technique within the design method in a world predicated on rapid change rather than stable tradition.

5. The Esoteric Turn of Theory

By the 1970s, theoretical writing on architecture began an inward philosophical turn, seeking foundations within language itself. The philosophy of structuralism came into its own in the 1960s, positing that all cultural systems have underlying structures that underpin their ability to convey meaning, and if language was recognized most visibly as a set of symbols that could communicate meaning, other symbolic systems also applied similar means. A linguistic analogy began to be applied to architecture, fashion, and many other artistic disciplines. A new architectural movement, which came to be known as postmodernism (for lack of a better name), sought to build itself on learning lessons from the past, believing that these carried symbolic cultural significance relevant to the present. One branch of this movement critiqued the abstractions of twentieth-century modernism, acknowledged public nostalgia for traditional architecture, and sought an architectural language that would creatively deploy a vocabulary of traditional elements from the past. Another branch—which sought to be less literal in its use of tradition—sought underlying typological principles from history that could then be filtered through the lens of a modernist aesthetic.[9]

This represented a third major turn in theory, one that began to create a widening gulf between theory and practice, for the earlier two turns had broader roots in the general social and political context. The Beaux-Arts model of a return to sacred origins took place in a milieu that was still largely traditional and religious, and the Bauhaus model of social idealism took place in an era where the creation of the democratic welfare state was in its formative years. These roots allowed the language of practice to hold a close correspondence with the language of theory, and what an architect might openly think and say within the routines of practice was not far removed from the way debates within academia were phrased. Once transcendental belief and social idealism were abandoned, and once theory began to ground itself in esoteric philosophical debate on the structure of language and other symbolic systems, the languages of architectural theory and everyday practice began to diverge. An architect who wished to engage with theory was reduced to discussing it only with other architects or academics.

The linguistic analogy in architectural theory became unraveled within the philosophy of language itself, falling into disfavor when the post-structuralist philosophy of deconstruction attacked its very foundations. Deconstruction critiqued and demolished what until then was a core assumption regarding language and symbolic systems in general: the metaphysics of presence and the assumption that any language pointed to a fixed meaning or truth. In any symbolic system of signs, any sign holds its meaning in relationship to other signs in the system. For example, the word "warm" does not refer to a fixed temperature but conveys meaning in terms of its position in the scale of "scalding, hot, warm, tepid, cold, and freezing." Thus, any sign never fixes meaning but only defers that meaning to other signs, and any text can be deconstructed to undermine the hierarchies it initially posited as axiomatic.

The philosophy of deconstruction is complex and beyond the scope of this essay, but it demolished the long-standing assumption that every symbolic system identifies fixed truths, arguing that any prescriptive philosophy or canonical axiom emerges more from ideology than any metaphysics of presence. Being primarily a mode of textual analysis, deconstruction is not directly applicable to architecture, but architects used its claims to validate a creative formalism—unconstrained by rectitude—that could even question fundamental compositional axioms such as orthogonal geometries. With the design process liberated by new possibilities in digital production, architectural creativity began to be judged by how out-of-the-box it was.

6. Architecture's Metamorphosis Under the Digital Revolution

This claimed freedom was shortly followed by transformational technological change—the emergence of satellite television and the internet toward the end of the twentieth century, followed by the explosion of social media in the first two decades of the twenty-first century—leading to a global circulation of seductive, provocative, and attention-grabbing visual images and videos at a scale and velocity never seen before. If Victor Hugo's concern was architecture being subsumed by the printed word, the word came under a similar displacement by the new ubiquity of digital visuality. This led to an increasing prevalence of aesthetic evaluation being reduced to snap judgment based on visual appeal, leading to three further transformations.

First, as Manuel Castells, sociologist and author, has pointed out, the digital revolution led to a new form of globalization where, for the first time, distant locations could be coordinated in real time, leading to a world characterized by non-local geographies representing a "space of flows" displacing an earlier world of a "space of places" where local geographies were dominant.[10] This author, in his practice, has had the experience of presenting a design to the chief executive of a software company in India only to realize that there was a greater concern over how the building would be perceived in California (where most of the company's clients were) than from across the street.

The second impact of the digital revolution was that the volume of information the average person was subjected to had risen exponentially. As the Nobel Prize-winning economist and political scientist Herbert Simon remarked, "In an information-rich world, the wealth of information means a dearth of something else: a scarcity of whatever it is that information consumes. What information consumes is rather obvious: it consumes the attention of its recipients. Hence a wealth of information creates a poverty of attention and a need to allocate that attention efficiently among the overabundance of information sources that might consume it."[11] This led to a global economy where one of the scarcest resources became attention, and the necessity to capture attention became one of the key factors shaping the economy.[12] This has led to a death of what had hitherto been a cutting edge of aesthetic production: the avant-garde. Two major means of capturing attention are scale and novelty. We see scale in the rising prevalence of business monopolies and large projects, and the avant-garde is seen as a valuable resource for mining novelty, with the work being detached from its critical foundations to foreground its attention-grabbing visual novelty. Thus, we see architects like Frank Gehry and Zaha Hadid, whose writings early in their careers constructed an identity of iconoclastic rebellion, quickly co-opted to become vehicles of mainstream capitalist branding.

Third, the increasing penetration of media exposure, with a media screen in almost every person's pocket, led to people viewing the world through the lens of media rather than embodied encounters with it. This led to what Daniel Boorstin presciently predicted in 1962—the appearance of an event in the media would take on greater weight than the reality of the event itself; a system revolving around celebrities, where a celebrity is defined as "a person who is known for his well-knownness."[13] This has led to a public perception of visually seductive architecture, where the cutting edge is increasingly tied to a mediatized cult of star architects, with the remaining majority of architects struggling to resist condemnation to a world of commoditized production.

7. Looking Ahead: Conceptualizing Reflective Practice

This set of deep challenges accumulated by history is what critical writing in architecture faces today: a loss of status as the "mother of the arts," other media taking over as the register of human thought, increasing degrees of abstraction, a growing divide between theory and practice, a loss of commonly held transcendental anchors, thoughtful reflection getting displaced by visual seduction, the increasing impact of non-local geographies in a digitized world, the death of the avant-garde as a creative cutting edge, and a world where media presence overwhelms lived reality. This is a heavy burden to bear, and the only way to escape its weight is to begin with fundamentals: if writing speaks for the voice of critical theory, it is necessary to start by seeking clarity on the relationship between theory and practice.

Donald Schön, philosopher and urban planning professor, acknowledged a gulf between the two (which prevails in other fields as well), pointing to a crisis of confidence in professional knowledge, where prevailing assumptions on the theory-practice connection do not reflect the way effective professionals function.[14] Schön defined the dominant assumption as the Model of Technical Rationality, where theory is seen as foundational to practice. One first develops a theory and subsequently applies it in practice, so practice is fundamentally an act of applied theory. Schön argued that the average professional project is too unique and complex a challenge to be reducible to applied theory. Effective professionals develop a value-based mastery of their craft and then use the professional challenge as a means of extending and expanding this mastery. The Model of Technical Rationality assumes a mode of "reflection and action," whereas effective professionals embody a capacity for "reflection in action."

Another way of framing this is to define theory and practice as activities that cover the same terrain, but in contrasting directions. Practice moves from the general to the particular: one starts from a general description such as a design brief, which leads to a set of conceptual possibilities, among which one option is then selected for development of a schematic design, after which the constructability of the design is examined, followed by managing the exigencies of construction. Each step in the process entails further degrees of detail, and if one does nothing but this, the trajectory of the process displaces the center of one's being toward the pole of detail to become the nuts-and-bolts architect who loses the forest for the trees. On the other hand, theory reverses this direction to move from the particular to the general, starting with a specific set of observations, seeking to extract underlying universal principles from them. Each step in this process entails further degrees of generalization, and if one does nothing but this, one's center of being shifts toward the pole of abstraction, tending toward the stereotypical ivory tower academic, distanced from the skills, methods, and mastery of professional practice. The two work best when one achieves balance by allowing them to contradict each other: theory becomes a mode for critiquing practice and practice a mode for critiquing theory. We have erred in largely segregating them into separate spaces, with theory assigned to academia and practice to design firms. We need more spaces where the two coexist, so that the critical interchange between them is institutionalized into daily life.

Theory and practice must converse with each other. We often make the error that we work our way through issues and challenges through linear chains of logic, whereas our actual progress develops through back-and-forth conversation. Conversation occurs even when we are alone. When an architect sketches to explore possibilities in design, every line drawn cannot be philosophized. Initially, philosophy retreats to the background and the sketch evolves through a tacit interchange between hand, eye, pencil, and paper. After a while, sketching stops, the pencil is put down, and the architect leans back to assess what has been drawn: the tacit interchange retreats to the background and philosophical critique steps into the foreground. After gaining something from this inversion, the pencil is lifted again to continue sketching, and the inversion repeats to send philosophy into the background once more. The sketch becomes a form of notation that allows a conversation to happen between design ideas and the architect proposing them, and the repeated inversion between philosophical critique and tacit action underpins this conversation. How valid a theory is and how foundational it is to practice is less important than the spaces and forms of notation that catalyze this conversation.

Ultimately, this dialog between theory and practice must aim at an introverted process of developing personal mastery within a reflective professional practice. This must be kept in mind in interpreting textual production, where theory, criticism, and history institutionalize writing as a specialized practice within the spaces of architectural academia and journalism. If we are to come to terms with what writing can offer architecture, our analysis must expand to this level too, and while one step would be to seek more spaces where theory and practice intermingle, we must also come to terms with what is involved when writing becomes a stand-alone endeavor.

8. Experience Versus Interpretation

An essay by landscape architect David Heymann raises the question of why the architect's creations stand out as singular creations in sharp contrast to the landscapes they inhabit, even in cases where landscape is cited as a primary source influencing the design.[15] One does not find this quality in vernacular architecture. In an argument based significantly on an essay by Loos,[16] Heymann debates that the relationship of a building to its landscape is not only visual, but also constitutional; it must play a part in sustaining a larger whole. But architecture is perceived as an art, and once art was transformed under modernism to privilege artistic innovation over transcendental belief, the creative intent of the architect was foregrounded to suggest that an architecture that must be interpreted before it is experienced. This differs from natural landscape and vernacular architecture, where natural landscape lacks a human creator and vernacular culture rests on the anonymity of artistic production, so interpretation can only be a by-product of experience. Loos is cited as arguing that architecture's primary role is to sustain culture rather than express art; culture is an ongoing experience rather than a singular interpretation, and by this measure, the farmer represents stronger roots in culture than the architect. Loos goes on to elaborate that there are only two building types where the inherent symbolism allows architecture to privilege art over culture: the monument and the tomb (here, one must recognize that Hugo's lament on printing overwhelming architecture is directed at architecture as monument), and all other architecture must submit to a constitutional obligation to context and landscape.

The privileging of interpretation is initially created by the modes of architectural education that privilege verbalization. The student is always next to her design and talking about it, either in a studio crit or defending it to a panel of critics. This breeds the assumption that the architect's intent, expressed through a voice that is always heard, is a primary generator of meaning and significance in architecture. William Saunders writes about his experience in an administrative position at the Graduate School of Design at Harvard University, United States, observing that students whose work starts from an idea that can be articulated are privileged, and those who cannot articulate such an idea—whose thinking cannot be separated from intuitive design choices—are categorized at a lesser level.[17] Saunders argues that when one is allowed to express an idea both verbally and visually, one can get away with mediocrity in both, whereas, when challenged to say something only verbally or only visually, one is challenged to be far more substantive.

The privileging of the architect's voice continues after the student graduates, sustained by criticism and journalism, leading to a culture where architects validate the intangible quality of their work through the social measure of peer review, assessing its reception in reputed professional journals and architecture schools, design competitions, invitations to the lecture circuit, or design awards won. While these are all valuable means of validation, when they become dominant, they breed a self-referential culture where architects are designing for other architects, failing to achieve sufficient clarity in recognizing the constituencies their projects are meant to serve.

An emphasis on interpretation fails to account for the inevitable silence of the architect, for once a project is completed and handed over for inhabitation, the architect disappears, never to be seen or heard from again, except in very rare exceptions. At this point, there is a culture of inhabitation that begins—one that breeds experiences and memories that are absorbed into the work over extended periods of time. Architecture must focus on the emancipatory potential in the culture of inhabitation it catalyzes, rather than privileging initial interpretation, for such interpretation—even when valued—will never survive the boredom of repetitive daily routine that most architecture is subjected to. Architecture, through its inhabitation, absorbs an aesthetic over time, and should base itself on aesthetics of absorption rather than the aesthetics of expression currently privileged in the profession.[18]

9. The Roles of Theory, Criticism, and History

Writing is inherently different from architecture as a mode of thought. It privileges linear interpretation over a multidimensional experience, the visual over the multi-sensory, and consequently, as Juhani Pallasmaa has so sensitively delineated,[19] valorizes focused perspectival vision that objectivizes space and distances the observer, while devaluing peripheral vision and the other senses that accentuate our experiential entanglement with, and immersion within, space. Theory, as an act of writing and speaking on architecture, is significant, even as a stand-alone, specialized activity, but must be valued for the critical and symbiotic conversation it unleashes with practice and the undesirable distortions it causes when privileged as philosophical or critical foundation.

Criticism and history also serve as counterpoints to practice but play different roles when compared to theory. Criticism offers a fresh viewpoint along third-person detachment, standing apart from the intimacy between architect and his/her creation. While often viewed as an act of explanation, explication, or judgment, its primary purpose is different, offering a gaze that can look through the appearance of a work to bring what it stands for into focus: a perspective best captured by Alan Colquhoun's statement, "Criticism occupies the no-man's land between enthusiasm and doubt, between poetic sympathy and analysis. Its purpose is not, except in rare cases, either to eulogize or condemn, and it can never grasp the essence of the work it discusses. It must try to get behind the work's apparent originality and expose its ideological framework without turning it into a mere tautology."[20]

Out of theory, criticism, and history—the three activities in which writing is central—history is perhaps seen as the most distant from practice, often believed to be a purely academic discipline; a perspective more pronounced after modernism redirected the architect's gaze from the past to the future. Architecture would do well to resurrect the intimacy between history and practice, not to revive the classical axiom that practice must found its compositions on historical precedent, but because the time span of the historical gaze is valuable. Heritage must not be seen as an authenticity from the past that we must carry into the future, but as a contemporary moment of critically assessing value that endures over time, to ascertain what is worth remembering, so that we may always hold it close to ourselves.[21] This long-duration perspective of time will provoke practice into not only considering what our ancestors can offer us, but also consider the ethical obligation upon us to be a good ancestor to the future.[22]

10. Conclusion: Translation and Poetry as Modes of Being and Practice

Ultimately, our analysis must not stay confined to a view of the role writing plays within architecture, for we must shake the narrowness of such a gaze that forgets that we are humans before we are architects, and must come to terms with this fact for "what is understood at this level could radically alter the juncture where we shift from our humanness into our professional avatars, consequently reshaping the discipline's terrain."[23] From this perspective, it is useful to study the literary modes by which we cope with the world, for such modes underpin our unavoidable compulsion, as sentient and reflexive beings, to translate knowing into telling. Two of these literary modes architecture would be well served to grant attention to are translation and poetry.

Joseph Rykwert suggests we view design as an act of translation.[24] We have the language of design process that deploys a vocabulary of ideas, sketches, drawings, models, and digital simulations. This holds no direct correspondence with the experiential and sensory language of inhabiting physical space over time. Design represents a translation from the language of process to the language of experience. Given that translation is an art far more than the mere deployment of dictionaries, it demands a significantly greater fluency in the language it's being translated into than the language it's being translated from. If I am to translate a poem from English into Hindi, I need enough English to appreciate the poem and its nuances, but I must be a masterful poet in Hindi. Poetic fluency in experiential inhabitation demands a priori rigorous interrogation of our own humanity; an interrogation that is foundational to our professional endeavors. But we tend to skip this interrogation and remain mired within the self-referential languages intrinsic to our profession. The poet's gaze is crucial to acquiring fluency in experience.

An often-cited quotation of Louis I. Kahn is: "A great building, in my opinion, must begin with the unmeasurable, go through measurable means when it is being designed, and in the end must be unmeasurable."[25] At first glance, this statement appears to be an oxymoron for it expects an ability to know, and consequently measure the immeasurable. But if one makes the necessary shift from the lens of interpretation to that of experience, we recognize that most of what makes life worthwhile (love, joy, beauty, wonder, and such similar awes) are impossible to measure, or define, but become known as unquestionably tangible reality when experienced. Since we cannot measure or directly describe these primordial realities, our only means of expressing them is either through embodied gesture or through poetic metaphor, and if we do not aim for fluency in either, we not only sanitize this value out of our lives, but in cutting ourselves off from this crucial way of being, we increase the burden the world places upon us.

Italian writer and journalist Italo Calvino speaks of how, when he first began to write, he felt a widening gulf between the lightness of good writing and the weight of the world he wished to write about.[26] The never-ending complexity and opacity of the world kept adding more to what he wanted to write, till he started to feel that the mass of the world was inducing in him an unavoidable petrification. On thinking this, he recalls the myth of Perseus, who is able to avoid the petrification entailed by Medusa's gaze and slay her by never looking at her directly but only at her reflection in a polished shield. Calvino sees in this myth an allegory for the poet's relationship with the world, never prioritizing the direct gaze of rationality which permits only the measurable self, but relying on the indirect gaze of metaphor that invokes the holistic self.

This is the lens with which we must examine writing. Observing it as an intellectual activity within the profession, we will be ill-served by privileging it as offering philosophical foundation, and will be better-served by treating it as a catalyst to the critical and energizing conversations between theory and practice. But even this is not enough. We must hold as paramount our obligation as professionals to translate architecture into life—remember, we are humans before we are architects—and pay heed to poet Robert Penn Warren's declaration that "what poetry most significantly celebrates is the capacity of man to face the deep, dark inwardness of his nature and his fate."[27]

We can never know architecture adequately without a rigorous and foundational quest to know ourselves.

Notes

1. Victor Hugo, "The Hunchback of Notre-Dame" in *The Works of Victor Hugo* (New York, United States: Black Readers Service Company, 1928), 169.
2. ibid, 170–180.
3. ibid, 177.
4. Alan Colquhoun, "The Beaux-Arts Plan," in *Essays in Architectural Criticism: Modern Architecture and Historical Change* (Massachusetts, United States: MIT Press, 1981), 161–168.
5. Walter J. Ong, *Orality and Literacy: The Technologizing of the Word* (London, United Kingdom: Methuen, 1982).
6. Joseph Rykwert, *The Brothers Adam: The Men and the Style* (London, United Kingdom: Collins, 1985).
7. Colquhoun, "The Beaux-Arts Plan," 168.
8. As a representative text, see Amos Rapoport, *House Form and Culture* (New Jersey, United States: Prentice-Hall, 1969).
9. Anthony Vidler, "The Third Typology," *Oppositions*, 7 (Winter 1976): 1–4.
10. Manuel Castells, *The Rise of the Network Society, The Information Age: Economy, Society and Culture, Vol. I* (Oxford, United Kingdom: Blackwell, 1996).
11. Herbert A. Simon, "Designing Organizations for an Information-Rich World" in *Computers, Communication, and the Public Interest*, ed. Martin Greenberger (Maryland, United States: The Johns Hopkins Press, 1971), 40–41.
12. Thomas H. Davenport and John C. Beck, *The Attention Economy: Understanding the New Currency of Business* (Massachusetts, United States: Harvard Business School Press, 2001).
13. Daniel J. Boorstin, *The Image: A Guide to Pseudo Events in America* (New York, United States: Harper, 1962).
14. Donald A. Schon, *The Reflective Practitioner: How Professionals Think in Action* (New York, United States: Basic Books, 1983).
15. David Heymann, "A Mound in the Wood," *Places Journal* (December 2011), https://doi.org/10.22269/111205.
16. Adolf Loos, "Architecture," in *On Architecture*, trans. Michael Mitchell (California, United States: Ariadne Press, 2002), 73–85.
17. William S. Saunders, "Architectural Education: Current Confusions – Is Architecture Allegory, Craft, or Art," *Architectural Record* 6 (May 1986): 49–51.
18. Prem Chandavarkar, "Notes on the Aesthetics of Absorption" (paper presentation, disContinuous Threads: Memory, Freedom, and Architecture in Contemporary India Conference, Mumbai, India, December 10–12, 1997), https://www.academia.edu/33252568/Notes_on_the_Aesthetics_of_Absorption_pdf.
19. Juhani Pallasmaa, *The Eyes of the Skin: Architecture and the Senses* (West Sussex, United States: John Wiley & Sons, 2005).
20. Alan Colquhoun, "From Bricolage to Myth, or How to Put Humpty-Dumpty Together Again," in *Essays in Architectural Criticism: Modern Architecture and Historical Change* (Massachusetts, United States: MIT Press, 1981), 169.
21. Prem Chandavarkar, "What is Heritage?" *Musings on Architecture & Urbanism*, May 13, 2017, https://premckar.wordpress.com/2017/05/13/what-is-heritage/.
22. Roman Krznaric, *The Good Ancestor: How to Think Long Term in a Short-Term World* (London, United Kingdom: Penguin Random House, 2020).
23. Prem Chandavarkar, "The Human Within the Architect" (paper presentation, The Frame Conclave on Modern Heritage, National Institute of Oceanography, Goa, India August 16–18, 2019), https://premckar.wordpress.com/2019/08/21/the-human-within-the-architect/.
24. Joseph Rykwert, "Translation and/or Representation," *Anthropology and Aesthetics*, vol. 34 (September 1998): 64–70.
25. Louis I. Kahn, quoted in Wilder Green, "Louis I. Kahn, Architect: Alfred Newton Richards Medical Research Building," *Museum of Modern Art Bulletin* 28, no. 1 (1961):3.
26. Italo Calvino, "Lightness," in *Six Memos for the Next Millenium* (New York, United States: Vintage Books, 1993), 3–30.
27. Robert Penn Warren, *Democracy and Poetry* (Massachusetts, United States: Harvard University Press, 1976), 31.

Figure Credits

Figure 1: Inner pages of *Ten Books on Architecture* by Marcus Pollio Vitruvius, the first illustrated edition published by Fra Giovanni Giocondo in 1511 (https://www.metmuseum.org/art/collection/search/367494, open access)
Figure 2: New Inventions of Modern Times [Nova Reperta], *The Invention of Book Printing*, plate 4 (Public domain of The Metropolitan Museum of Art Collection, https://www.metmuseum.org/art/collection/search/659683).
Figure 3: Cuneiform, Egyptian, and Chinese writings at different times by various processes [J. De Morgan, *Note sur les procédés techniques en usnge chez les scribes babyloniens*, In: Maspero Gaston, *Recueil de travaux relatifs à la philologie et à l'archéologie égyptiennes et assyriennes*, vol. 27 (Paris, Libr. Honoré Champion, 1870), 243, public domain].

How to Believe in Architecture becoming an Author of History

Ole BOUMAN, College of Architecture and Urban Planning, Tongji University

Ole Bouman is a Dutch-German cultural historian, art historian, and archeologist. He is Professor at Tongji University and the Founding Director Emeritus of Design Society (the new design museum and platform in Shenzhen, now in the sixth year of its full operation and listed by *Time* magazine as being among the World's 100 Greatest Places). Past roles include editor-in-chief of *Volume* (a magazine he co-founded with OMA and Columbia University; 2005–2007) and director of the Netherlands Architecture Institute (NAi; 2006–2013). He worked as a curator for Manifesta 3 (2000), and curated national pavilions at the Biennales of Shenzhen, São Paulo and Venice. He was Creative Director of the Urbanism/Architecture Bi-City Biennale Shenzhen (UABB) in 2013–2014. His publications include *The Invisible in Architecture* (co-author, 1994), *Ubiquitous China* (2006), *Architecture of Consequence* (2009) and *Design Society: the Making of a New Creative Platform* (co-editor, 2017). Bouman taught architecture and design at the Massachusetts Institute of Technology and the University of Hong Kong. In 2018 he received the Shenzhen Creative Influencer Award.

Abstract

Architecture and writing, two of the longest-standing expressions of human civilization, have been intertwined since their inception. Writing has touched upon, promoted, covered, commented, responded to, and reviewed architecture. It has also explored architecture's assumed essentials, putting them in theories and manifestos. Many writers have challenged architecture and inspired its practice. Some have even reached such levels of authority as to begin guiding architecture, and determine its most important legacy. At a critical point, the passive and reactive stance of writing—waiting for physical reality to manifest itself first—turns into a leading role of defining destinies, mandates, and agendas. This essay reflects on this cultural history, exemplifying it through the personal experience of the author across decades of writing, editing, designing, and curating. It ends with a call to participate, in an effort to eventually merge writing and architecture into a new cultural practice.

Author Information
Ole BOUMAN: boumanole@tongji.edu.cn

Keywords

Architecture, writing, integration, culture, civilization, history, new directions.

1. Introduction

This special issue of *Architecture Asia*, devoted to the theme of writing and literature, comes at a special time. Writing, as evidenced by the recent launch of the many varieties of new artificial intelligence applications, is no longer what it used to be: the exclusive domain of a strong mind capable of grasping a thought, articulating it, and putting it into an argument. These foundations of writing are at now stake, now that the computer needs only "prompts" to produce seemingly coherent pieces, drawing from the infinite amount of "content" available in the data ocean. In the age of ChatGPT, that which until recently passed for plagiarism—the copying of another's thoughts and formulations without citing sources—is no longer a mortal sin. However, letting the computer combine infinite thoughts and formulations also heralds a whole new chapter in the history of writing, and with the expected improvements of these chatbots, it will probably come to a level where even "prompts" are no longer necessary, which will most likely be the end of historiography itself. For it is not just text production that is changing. It is primarily the outsourcing of text interpretation that will cause the inner drive and motivation to write to disappear, giving way to reasons like needing to make a deadline or generate and income, or wanting to establish a reputation be the purpose[1] for using AI applications like ChatGPT.

Unless... just maybe, it turns out that the will to write something outstanding and something that no one else has thought of yet, and above all, something that becomes authentic and convincing because of the personal urge of the writer, will turn out to be stronger than laziness, and even stronger than the fervent desire—known to every writer—to escape the struggle to complete a good text.

2. Writing for Writing's Sake

(Everything that follows in this essay assumes this possibility of "unless.")
Let's assume that it still makes sense to ponder the power of writing and explore what it still can do. However, even if that idea is the starting point, we are far from finished, given the inclination to convenience, which has always manifested itself amply in writing.

Slightly less recent than an intelligent chatbot, but already amply defined by time constraints, impulse behavior, vanity, and algorithmic triggers, is the writing culture of ultra-short pieces on social media. Many have made a habit of "posting"—be it opinions or otherwise—as a daily routine. To all these people who fight for a prime spot on other people's social media "timelines," a variety of platforms, formats, and marketing techniques are available, which blur the line between what is said and what is "posted." The demand for high frequency, or perhaps the addiction to it, is causing a steady erosion of stylistic ability in even the most prominent writers. A bad book will gnaw at you for a lifetime, whereas a lame Tweet can happen to anyone. Ironically, that bad Tweet will probably be of better service in the quest for name recognition; even more so than an excellent book might. Now, who can resist that perverse logic?

3. Writing about Architecture

Leaving the dynamics of authorship, as such, to steer the discussion more precisely toward the topic of architecture, one notes that there, too, the metastasis of non-committal text manifests itself—but it is interesting to see how it relates to the importance and urgency of architecture as a social necessity. And how this importance is reflected in the written word.

While there is a genre titled "architecture"—which seems to be about architecture—it can sometimes be hard to grasp why, for countless are the books and articles that add little to architecture, being merely casuistic descriptions, articulations, specifications, or at best, commentaries. It seems like an arbitrary topic choice; stuff which would never have been published without something that happened prior to the writing—merely writing as a response to the physical reality that precedes it.

Often, it seems like it might as well be another reality which the writer is responding to. This type of writing may help the professional conversation about architecture and the dialog between architects; it remains a way to remain updated, but for culture, or even society as a whole, this type of passive writing is hardly significant. For real substance, you need a certain degree of abstraction that arises from or contributes to a bird's-eye view. Additionally, you need an intellectual drive.

4. Writing on Architecture

Which writing has that?

There is a type of writing that puts architecture itself—its status, its mandate, its crises, and its glory—at the center. This brings us to a number of famous writers who had the courage and ability to speak out about quality in architecture; who dared to use common denominators, and who were able to transcend the empirics to formulate a vision. These authors include Sir Banister Flight Fletcher,[2] Sir Nikolaus Pevsner,[3] and Bruno Zevi.[4] On a more recent timeline is the work of Kenneth Frampton,[5] whose survey work, *Modern Architecture: A Critical History*, taught generations of architecture students their first general professional awareness. Another example is Charles Jencks, who in his famous diagrams gave all kinds of movements, trends, and oeuvres a place in an apparently knowable historical reality.[6] The Belgian architecture critic Geert Bekaert devoted a lifetime cultivating "the conversation about architecture,"[7] always seeking the connection between an architectural project and historical and cultural themes. He also ran journals and operated an architecture bookstore. Bekaert's intellectual legacy continues through students such as Hilde Heynen[8] and Christophe van Gerrewey,[9] representing perhaps the most architecture-discursive nation in the world—that of the Flemings.

Practicing architects, often too close to projects to be able to muster the necessary detachment for a historical overview, have also sometimes compiled their overarching insights into the meaning of architecture into tractate-like publications. Adolf Loos, in *Ins Leere Gesprochen*[10] analyzed the fate of architecture (and other expressions of culture) and connected them with cultural criticism. One hundred years later, this tradition is represented by architects like Herman Hertzberger,[11] Peter Zumthor[12] and Yung Ho Chang,[13] who try to put their personal experiences and insights into lessons others can learn from.

With them should also be mentioned Rem Koolhaas, probably the most prolific architect/author of the last half of the century, whose position has always been between writing and designing, and whose fame depends in no small measure on his ability to analyze and put into words the fate of architecture itself.

5. Writing to Set a Standard

All these authors have reached a level where writing is no longer a derivative of a so-called built reality. Their texts have an independent persuasive power that makes sense even without building, or which precede building and may become a source of inspiration for it. Loos even wrote a text that reads like a crucial rhetorical choice: *Ornament and Crime*.[14] This is a writing that begins with fundamental reflection and only after, then asks how architecture can respond to it; this form in its intellectual clarity makes a compelling case for design to account for, so as to become sharper and better. Here, writing becomes a form of intellectual leadership within the entire discipline. It is no longer about architecture, but *for* architecture.

One writes as an expression of a spatial ideal, to which architecture becomes the vehicle. One writes to raise an agenda proposal for all culture.

This kind of writing about architecture takes architecture much further than building alone ever can. The meaning, mandate, and power—in short, the value of architecture—is established by writers. Intellectual authority, as well as historical relevance, sometimes even receive great recognition by practitioners. They, too, eventually recognize that the milestones of their profession—which they share and recognize as their canon—are books, reversing the famous quote from Victor Hugo's *The Hunchback of Notre Dame: "Ceci inspirera cela"* (This will inspire that).

Now, we come to the yardsticks of architectural history: *The Ten Books on Architecture* by Vitruvius,[15] *Yingzao Fashi: Treatise on Architectural Methods or State Building Standards* (营造法式) by Li Jie,[16] *De Re Aedificatoria* by Alberti,[17] and *Towards an Architecture* by Le Corbusier.[18] They are manifestos on the essence of good architecture that are not intended to explain one's own work, but to set a standard for many.

6. Writing to Set an Agenda

There is another genre of texts about architecture, which leads it away from the center of the argument. These texts are about the world and the core values of society, with necessarily enormous architectural consequences. Architecture in these sources is no longer a subject, but a dimension to express something in.

The Bible has many architectural moments and demonstrates an intense architectural sense of structure, construction, suspense, punch line, spatial control, and dramatic site selection. Or how could Johann Sebastian Bach's famous oratorio, *St. Matthew Passion*, exist without architecture, both in the story itself and the manner in which it sets out the chapters of the Gospel of Matthew to music?

Karl Marx's *Das Kapital* brings an awareness of architecture—both as a means of production and its outcome—and thus of the power relations that determine what architecture looks like and who owns space, land, materials, and even time. The current United Nations-led Intergovernmental Panel on Climate Change (IPCC) reports are contemporary variants of these universal texts, with inescapable consequences for architecture. These texts can be seen as messages to humanity. Architecture as the physical manifestation of our civilization can't ignore the call for purpose and must reflect on its future. Where do we profess faith, and how do we shape that environment? Where is the place for community, and do we create added value for public? How do we provide a generative environment that will no longer be based on the extraction of our planetary resources. Hence, these publications that are meant for everyone are also meant for architects. And they (architects)—because of their specific responsibilities and ability—can do much more with them.

7. Architecture to Structure Writing

And so, we now come to where writing on, for, and at the service of architecture turns into architecture as an inevitable consequence of writing, or architecture becoming an alternative form of writing.

The works of Laozi, Plato, St. Augustine, Bernard of Clairvaux, Descartes, and Freud had immeasurable impact on people's minds, and hence on the spaces around them. Sometimes, the architectural dimension was expressed in their book titles.[19]

There are a few examples of architects who translated the books of these great minds directly into their work, but often, a translation into architectural theory was first needed. It is not difficult to locate the monuments from the general cultural history in the history of architecture, and often, architectural theorists have helped make this relationship even more evident. From analyses of the deeper cultural significance of spatial effects, such as light play, enclosing, routing, scale, proportion and so on, to sometimes even complete blueprints of a new utopian world.

8. Architecture Becomes the Writing of History

Thus, the relationship between writing and design continues to expand and also overlap more and more. The further intertwining of the two are conceivable, each of which rises above writing as a specific activity, such that it arrives at a metaphorical level in which both writing about and designing architecture become a way of speaking about creating a meaningful life.

First, is the handful of architects in history who no longer saw their work as the spatial organization of a program, but as a vehicle for writing history itself. This is (acceptably) a dubious genre, in which hubris lurks. Most architects who practice this genre are satisfied with the paper version of history. Think of Étienne-Louis Boullée's cenotaph for Isaac Newton, or Bruno Taut's Die Stadtkrone or El Lissitzky's Prounenraum—architectural ideals that anticipate future perfection that will never come; it's architecture as an alternative manifesto.

Second, is how a linguistic relationship between text and architecture can be established. Not only at the level of plots and structures in stories and tracts, but even at the level of sentences and words architecture is recognizable. One can think of the use of the preposition to express meaning by structuring text through spatial units. But in Chinese, for example, the characters for these prepositions can themselves be read as architecture. Slowly but surely, the two aspects—writing and architecture— of this essay lose their own distinctiveness and merge with each other.

9. Belief in Discourse

Now that this essay has gone into such detail about the intense, even symbiotic, relationship between architecture and writing, it has come time for me to hold myself personally accountable. This essay was not written as the result of an arbitrary neutral investigation. On the contrary, it is based on my own experiences throughout my career—often full of harm to myself; sometimes also providing great pleasure.

I have written several books in my life, and a multitude of essays, reviews, editorials, and other forms of reflection. Most of the content in these writings is about architecture, in all degrees of substance, and certainly architecture in the broadest sense of the word. Yet, not so broad that they lose their subject matter and focus. All these pieces—spanning decades—touch on, encircle, and present/frame architecture in such a way as to imply that we have some idea of what it is. I have used many definitions of it, old and new, known and unknown: "The Mother of the Arts," "The most generalist and comprehensive human activity," "The most expensive art," and "The organization of space." Counting the word "architecture" in just the titles of my publication would yield a respectable number. Apparently, all along, I believed in the importance of writing about architecture.

But I didn't just write myself. I also, as an editor of magazines, compiler of collections, organizer of lectures and conferences, asked others to write and organize thoughts, perhaps almost a thousand times over. So apparently, I also believed in the role of debate and discourse. And now, as I commit these words to the page, I am once again demonstrating that. At least, that is what you, the reader, no doubt assume.

10. From Discourse to Action

Yet in the development of that belief in the power of words, much has happened over time. Of course, there is the development from student to teacher, and thus a movement from study to the sharing of knowledge. But there is also a development from writing as a secondary reaction to a reality that presents itself, to writing as an attempt to generate a new reality and propose new opportunities. From reaction to proposition, from journalism to agenda setting. That may sound very progressive and courageous, but often, both yield equally dramatic results in terms of public impact: from the journalist who tries to be there as early as possible (without ever creating themselves) to the guide who proposes a path to a destination that hardly anyone is interested in (yet). Behold, the fate of the writer on architecture, as I know them all too well: he or she is either too late, or too early. Can writing ever be exactly on time?

I retraced this path a few years ago by launching a digital archive of all important publications, re-presented as arguments in a topical discourse about our current state in the world.[20] The material is organized in such a way that a mandate of architecture emerges: not architecture as an end in itself, but as a means of understanding the world, giving it form and direction, and even the decisiveness to actually realize that form and direction. The whole reflects two qualities of architecture that I have always valued the most. First, that of the diagnosis of our time and second, as the most complete medium for following up on the diagnosis with the appropriate treatment. That this also gives you a roof over your head is a nice fringe benefit.

11. From Diagnosis to Therapy

This dual potential role of architecture is again reflected in two articles recently added to this archive, each highlighting one side of the issue.

The diagnosis part is phrased in bleak terms; it does not look good.

The Solipsism of Architecture[21]:

"(...) Irrespective of a growing existential awareness of the need for system change on the periphery of architecture and beyond, there is one thing that does not appear to succumb to any historical imperative whatsoever: the tendency to begin by interpreting everything that happens in the world in terms of architecture. Whatever the crisis, there will be no action before due consideration has been given to what the situation means for architecture. And 'for the role of the architect.' In other words, what prevails is the egocentric question of 'what's in it for me?' The entire system can topple, ecology can collapse, the world can founder, but architecture's first concern will always be about what will happen to itself. First find out 'what design can do.' First report back to the professional community. First evaluate the consequences for the 'curriculum,' or the 'title,' or the definition of architecture. And if it all gets too complicated, there'll be statements that 'not too much should be expected' of design, that social crises fall outside the curriculum, or do not fall within the definition of architecture. Group protection is always infinitely stronger than species protection. What remains are the reflections of the do-gooder. Interesting questions, subtle considerations, a residuum of self-doubt. But when the time comes for deeds, they look a hell of a lot like the deeds of old.

Over 20 years since the Kyoto Protocol, over 10 years since the Global Financial Crisis, and in the first year after the global Coronavirus pandemic, there has been no real change in the architecture of architecture itself. That will only happen when it stops connecting everything with itself, stops beginning with itself. When it admits the revolution into its own citadel."

A treatment proposal, however, is phrased in hopeful words.

Architecture as a Medium of Change[22]:

"Let's reconceive Africa... to a land still to be invented. A land that embodies and exemplifies the system change that the whole world needs. A continent that can be regenerating itself, without the carbon emissions, plastic pollutions, unsustainable extractions, and human caused species extinctions as we know it. A continent that brims with ideas to leapfrog from being victimized to the interest of others, to its own enlightened leadership.

As Lesley Lokko says (presenting the chief curatorial concept for the Venice Biennale 2023 that positions 'Africa as laboratory of the future'), 'Architects historically are key players in translating images into reality.'

I think architecture can do much more. Rather than starting with images, with rhetoric and noble intentions, it can be a medium of change itself, relevant for the many, not the few. Rather than translating, it's about creating a new kind of discipline beyond the scale of small individual projects, individual signatures, and reputations. Good design provides direction, can lead us on the road toward a highly necessary alternative spatial fix, which is both good for the African people and for humanity.

Let's bring the power of architecture to the stage that counts, and let architecture show its great strengths to be part of Africa's progress."

Diagnosis and therapy—this two-sided approach to architecture has defined my work for a long time. From one speaks the words of Antonio Gramsci: a "pessimism of the mind." From the other, an "optimism of the will." Given the plight of our existential situation, architecture could play a key role through a unified exploration, and then application, of an entirely different spatial organization of life on our planet. However, it essentially plays a role in its demise now. Use of

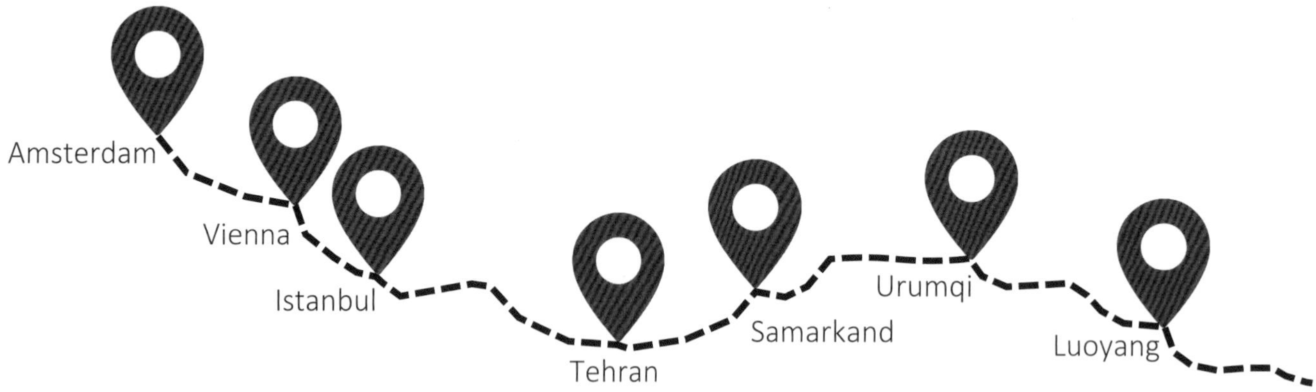

Figure 1
Tracing a new Silk Road of Architecture from Europe to Asia

non-renewable resources, spatial fixations by which we increase climate risks for decades to come, and waste of talent and absolute subservience to those who manage our planet very badly largely determine our contemporary architectural production.

The warning and the proposal—culturally, both schools of thought are important, against pride and procrastination; pro faith in our true potential. But I believe we may also note that both avenues of future action are currently largely ignored by the field. For myself, at least, this denial had major personal consequences.

12. Exile as a Consequence

This is not the place to go into detail about these personal consequences. For the sake of my argument, let one example suffice.

In 2009, as director of the Netherlands Architecture Institute, I published a book, together with several collaborators, entitled *Architecture of Consequence*, calling on architecture to focus on the major issues of our time.[23] These are issues that have only become more urgent since then: climate, energy, food supply, public health, social cohesion, and the waste of our most important life resources: space, and time.

The book also contained a collection of examples of an alternative architecture that responded to those issues. The book was thus a diagnosis and resolution at the same time and became for myself, the explicit guide for my directorate. Exhibitions, conferences, incubation projects and international collaborative projects followed. Even the building of the Institute was transformed to upgrade it to higher standards of ecological and social sustainability. *Architecture of Consequence* became the framework for a structural move from warnings to solutions, as a comprehensive value proposition to the entire professional community.

To my surprise, that same community went on a counter-offensive. The national government and funding agency did not like this activation of public money to non-artistic motives and eventually moved to dissolve the Architecture Institute as part of a large institutional overhaul. Schools, professional organizations, and prominent figures allowed it to happen in silence. And I myself became criticized for not only expecting far too much from architecture, but for implicitly accusing the design world of complicity in the untenable status quo. The result was extreme defensiveness. These experiences, taken together, brought an end to my activities at home and the beginning of an ongoing exile, to this day, to Asia, particularly China, where from day one, I experienced a great curiosity about new roles for architecture and design, and the ensuing social benefits it may have.

I went, in other words, on a journey. One could say that the provisional terminus of this personal development is the invitation to write this essay in *Architecture Asia*. But what next?

Although the profession's getting cold feet having realized its own role in an age of crisis and the following numbing of its mandate had profound implications for myself, the mechanism is far from new. Architectural history has numerous examples of rejection of radical reflection on its risks and dangers. Construction, traditionally based on practical ingenuity, craft and technical know-how, and relying largely on the goodwill of capital, has a long anti-intellectual tradition. Architectural critics have known the feeling of being wanted, only if they serve as respectable marketers of architects who set the agenda. If they are critical, or even agenda makers themselves, other mechanisms come into play. Usually, they are parked in academia and can pass their knowledge to students who have no reputation to lose yet. If they are not satisfied with that and want to participate in the public debate, condescension, opposition, and marginalization may follow.

You will have to motivate yourself as a writer to continue in a more sovereign way than by hoping for recognition. And this may be found in something more than just writing. Can it be found completely outside the comfort zone of professional dogmas, codes, and conventions? Is it possible to create a whole new framework for architectural intelligence? To be beyond or not be, that's the question.

13. Journey

So here comes my proposal for *Architecture Asia* readers: since you predominantly live and work across the Eurasian continent, can we write a song line together, that follows the permutations of landmass, nations, and cultural borderlines? Can we discover a Silk Road of Architecture together, that connects the most creative communities? Can we design a journey which meanders like, so to speak, a promenade *continentale*?

As this journey goes way beyond the boundaries of any architecture as we know it, with clients and budgets and construction sites, it may manifest itself in borders to cross, doors to open, details to be seen, and much more. And by revealing all these intricacies of cultures, languages, value systems, tastes, and countless other subjectivities, an architecture may come to the fore to connect like no architecture ever did before. An extended architecture that will be discovered, rather than imposed; with elements that will be hunted and gathered rather than extracted and produced. If this may succeed, writing will provide the score of the melody, the choreography of the dance, and the script of the movement. It is such a journey that will intertwine architecture and writing as mediums for explorations and exchanges (Figure 1, page 16).

Let me know if you are interested. And if successful, I promise to rewrite this essay in the reverse direction.

Acknowledgment

This essay is built on the shoulders of many other writers, whose relentless pursuit of clarity I'm greatly indebted to. With some of them, I had the privilege to discuss the relationship between writing and architecture explicitly and relentlessly, most notably Arjen Oosterman, my colleague at *Archis* magazine for many years.

Notes

1. For a now somewhat comical exploration of the consequences, see https://archinect.com/news/article/150344649/archinect-appoints-chatgpt-as-its-new-editor-in-chief.
2. Banister Fletcher, *Global History of Architecture* (London, United Kingdom: Bloomsbury, 21st edition, 2019).
3. Nikolaus Pevsner, *An Outline of European Architecture* (London, United Kingdom: Thames & Hudson, revised edition, 2019).
4. Bruno Zevi, *Storia Dell'Architettura Moderna* (Rome, Italy: Biblioteca Enaudi, revised edition 2004).
5. Kenneth Frampton, *Modern Architecture: A Critical History* (London, United Kingdom: Thames & Hudson, 5th edition, 2020).
6. Charles Jencks, *The Language of Postmodern Architecture* (New York, United States: Rizzoli, 1977).
7. Geert Bekaert, *Verzamelde Opstellen* (Antwerp, Belgium: WZW Editions & Productions, 2010).
8. Hilde Heynen et al., *Dat is architectuur. Sleutelteksten uit de twintigste eeuw* (Rotterdam, The Netherlands: NAi/010 Publishers, 2001).
9. Christophe van Gerrewey, *OMA Rem Koolhaas, A Critical Reader* (Basel, Switzerland: Birkhäuser, 2004).
10. Adolf Loos, *Ins Leere Gesprochen, 1897–1900* (Berlin, Germany: Der Sturm, 1921).
11. Herman Hertzberger, *Lessons for Students in Architecture* (Rotterdam, The Netherlands: NAi/010 Publishers, revised edition 2016).
12. Peter Zumthor, *Thinking Architecture* (Basel, Switzerland Birkhäuser, 2010).
13. Yung Ho Chang, *Design as Experience Research* (Victoria, Australia: The Images Publishing Group, 2023.
14. Adolf Loos, "Ornament and Crime", translated from Adolf Loos, "Ornament und Verbrechen," 1929. This essay was first composed in 1908 and formed the premise of a lecture by Loos in 1910 at Akademischer Verband für Literatur und Musik in Vienna, Austria.
15. Marcus Vitruvius Pollio, *Ten Books on Architecture* (Cambridge, United Kingdom: Cambridge University Press, revised edition, 1999).
16. Li Jie, *Yingzao Fashi* (Cambridge, United Kingdom: Cambridge University Press, revised edition, 2016).
17. Leon Battista Alberti, *Re Aedificatoria; On the Art of Building in Ten Books*, trans. by Joseph Rykwert, Robert Tavernor, and Neil Leach (Massachusetts, United States: MIT Press, 1988).
18. Le Corbusier, *Toward an Architecture*, trans. John Goodman (United States: Getty Research Institute, 2007).
19. St. Augustine, *The City of God* (Berlin, Germany: De Gruyter, revised edition, 1997).
20. The digital archive can be referred to www.olebouman.agency.
21. Ole Bouman, "The Solipsism of Architecture," https://www.olebouman.agency/post/the-solipsism-of-architecture.
22. Ole Bouman, "Architecture as a Medium of Change," https://www.olebouman.agency/post/architecture-as-a-medium-of-change.
23. Ole Bouman, *Architecture of Consequence* (Rotterdam, The Netherlands: NAi/010 Publishers, 2010).

Figure Credits

Figure 1: Tracing a new Silk Road of Architecture from Europe to Asia (author's diagram).

Indian Architectural Literature in UK's Academe: Exploring the Systemic Bias Against Indian Architecture and the Way Forward

Sumita SINGHA, Ecologic Architects

Sumita Singha is an architect, teacher, and writer with awards including UIA: UNESCO, Women In Business and Atkins Inspire awards. She received an OBE for services to architecture in 2021. She founded Architects For Change, the Equality forum at the Royal Institute of British Architects (RIBA), and is past Chair of Women In Architecture. She has served on RIBA committees for decades. Currently, she is a nationally elected RIBA Councillor and the Board Trustee for Education. Sumita Singha served as a non-executive Director in the UK's National Health Service (NHS) for nine years. She is a trustee of Architects Benevolent Society, Waltham Abbey Royal Gunpowder Mills and Commonwealth Association of Architects; and founding director of Charushila, an environmental design charity. She has also taught sustainable design for over 25 years and is an external examiner at several universities. Sumita Singha is the author of many books and articles on architecture, inclusion, coloniality, and women in architecture.

Abstract

This paper examines the systemic bias, ignorance, and occasionally, the deliberate rejection of Indian architecture within the Western academe. Many factors, such as colonial misappropriations, exoticization, anonymity of authorship of the work, and the syncretic nature of the forms leading to arbitrary categorizations have led to a scenario where Indian architecture—ancient and modern—has been ignored in academe, despite India holding cultural significance, which has influenced world architecture and culture. Indian architecture continues to be influenced by not only its colonial past but also by current movements. With the emergence of global associations (modern trade associations, research, and study) and connected problems (such as the climate and building materials crises), and the prevalence of the digital world, and secondary sources of education, access to knowledge repositories globally may become more equitable and progressive.

Author Information
Sumita SINGHA: contact@ecologicarchitects.com

Keywords

India, Asia, colonial, architecture, academe, literature, bias.

Source	Western Architectural Literature	Non-Western Architectural Literature	Reasons for selection
Google	134 million	75 million	Most popular search engine references
Amazon	More than 30,000	Less than 3,000	Online bookseller
Abe Books	14,300	670	Online book reseller
RIBA library	605	15	RIBA operates in 115 countries in various capacities
Architectural Association	218	6	Private school in London open to international students
London Metropolitan University	378	25	Has a Projects Office (established in 2004) to provide professional support for the delivery of live projects in places such as India and Nepal

Table 1
Comparison of architectural literature available on popular websites and educational institutions of the UK (carried out February 24, 2023)

1. Introduction

With the emergence of global associations (modern trade associations and research and study associations) and interconnected problems (such as the climate and building materials crises), and the acceptance of the digital world, the democratization and access to architectural collections, and the knowledge exchange between the East and the West should have become more equitable and progressive. Particularly, India as a major world economy, with a large English-speaking population,[1] should be difficult to ignore, especially as a past colony of the United Kingdom. However, that is not quite the reality.

The Indian subcontinent is home to all the major world religions and is the founding country of two of those religions: Hinduism and Buddhism. Religions have also contributed to architecture through their buildings, such as churches, synagogues, temples, mosques, tombs, and so on, along with related architectural and technical literature. Indian architecture has been, and continues to be, influenced by not only its colonial past but also by current expressions. The country is home to an impressive 379 architecture schools, including famous ones such as the Sir J J College of Architecture in Mumbai and the School of Planning and Architecture in Delhi. Architecture education is thriving in India, but the main references for Indian architects continue to be either Western or Western-derived.[2] This paper explores why this might be.

Writings on Indian architecture, art, and history need to have a diverse body of advocates and references, including native ones, not just Western. So, for this paper, quotes and learnings from Indian heritage writers or those based in India have been used because it is important that the people who come from a particular place can tell their own narrative and histories. The paper's main argument uses examples from Indian architecture, although reference is also made to other Asian thought leaders. In referring to India, the paper also refers to the Indian subcontinent as it was known during colonial times. We refer to the subject of architecture in the broadest sense, with all its entanglements, such as its sources, references and systems, specialized skills, jargon, codes of conduct, professional/public/academic institutions, education, practice, history, books, magazines (including those online), exhibitions (including those online), patronage, prominent personalities, mythical heroes (occasional heroines!), canonical buildings, installations, and now, social media.

1.1 The Non-Western Canon

First, let us examine the availability of Indian and non-Western architectural literature worldwide and in the UK. To understand how the UK's academe is supplied with architectural literature about the Indian subcontinent, an online survey of literature about Indian and non-Western architecture was carried out—the results of which are reproduced in Table 1 above. It is to be noted that a straightforward search for Indian architectural literature proved to be inconclusive. Inserting "Indian architecture" in the keywords section brought up books about native Americans. A search for "Non-Western" architecture books in Amazon.co.uk/Amazon.eu pulled up over 3,000 books, while "Indian architecture" totaled over 5,000 books; upon reviewing the results closely, many turned out to be about native American culture, fables, and such, not just architecture. In the search in the Architectural Association library database, although 300 titles were displayed, not all of them were about Indian

Figure 1
Marriage halls in Western style on a road in West Delhi

architecture. Some included other Asian, Middle Eastern and even South American architectural literature.

Many Indian students come to study in the UK, and many architects of Indian or Asian origin practice in the UK. According to the Architects Registration Board of the UK, Asian or Asian British people account for 8 percent of the Register, with Asians now representing 12 percent of the new entrants to the Register.[3] Three percent of architects on the UK Register are Asian or Asian British men, and 2 percent are Asian or Asian British women (Asians represent 9 percent of UK's population according to the latest census). Although it is not known how many Indian overseas study architecture specifically, the latest UK Immigration Statistics published show that nearly 118,000 Indian students received a student visa in the year ending June 2022—an 89 percent increase from the previous year, overtaking Chinese students.[4] These overseas students are taught using Western modalities, which are reproduced when they return home. According to the Commonwealth Architects Association's 2023 survey, there are approximately 670 faculties teaching architecture, over 400 of which are in India—a good proportion of which have been operational only for the past 10–15 years.

1.2 Curriculum, "Live" Academic Projects, and the Decolonization Movement

Apart from these statistics, there is an appetite for domestic non-Asian students to study Indian architecture. An example of such academic work would be the European Union (EU)-funded five-year Monsoon Assemblages project at the University of Westminster, London, United Kingdom; "Monsoonal Multiplicities is an exhibition of work arising from a five-year engagement with the monsoon[s] in India, Bangladesh, London, and Myanmar. It offers visitors a virtual experience of the monsoon by following stories of entangled beings, energies, infrastructures, life-worlds, matters, technologies, and knowledge practices and their mobilization by colonial and neo-colonial agendas."[5] London Metropolitan University, London, United Kingdom has a studio unit 6 —the "Architecture of Rapid Change and Scarce Resources," 'showcasing students' work about India[6] and Nepal, alongside other non-western countries. The library database search for "Indian architecture" of both institutions yielded about 655 and 280 entries respectively (including books and journals), many of which were not related to architecture. Most were written by Western authors, even including the works of James Fergusson, the 19th CE Scottish indigo plantation owner, and Percy Brown, the 19th CE English artist and art critic.[7] The library database search of the Architectural Association yielded 300 results for Indian architecture and had many commonalities with the other UK based institutions.

Despite the interest to study Indian and Asian architecture, the lack of recognition and unavailability of non-Western canons in education have led to student movements such as "Decolonize Education" and "Decolonizing Architecture" in the UK and US. In 2014, the National Architectural Accrediting Board (NAAB) in the US called for instruction in the history of architecture to include non-Western material and the Massachusetts Institute of Technology (MIT), United States, received a funding of $1million to do just that. However, other countries are still far behind on this issue. Many universities worldwide have begun teaching about non-Western architecture—like Carnegie Mellon University (United States), Northumbria University (England, United Kingdom),

University of Ulster (Northern Ireland), Cardiff University (Wales, United Kingdom) and Universities of Lincoln and Hull (England, United Kingdom), University of Santos Thomas (Philippines), University of California, Berkeley (United States), and National University of Athens (Greece)—but the syllabus is mostly limited to the Middle East or Byzantine architecture. Such decolonizing movements have not yet happened in the Indian architectural academe. But the Indian "anti-colonial nationalistic movements," as defined by Partha Chatterjee[8] and the 2020 reimagination of the Central Vista project in New Delhi, India, may be early indication of this decolonizing and may possibly flourish into a renewed understanding of the indigenous architecture of India. However, at present, there remains limited understanding of the relevance of Indian architecture in the UK's academe while popular culture in India idolizes Western architecture and culture (Figure 1, page 20).

1.3 Disregard of the Non-Western Canon: Two Examples

The lack of architectural literature about the Asian canon, the easy acceptance of this exclusion, and further, the dismissal of any need to examine this further or make up for it, is best reflected in the introduction in *Thinking about Architecture: An Introduction to Architecture Theory* by Colin Davies, who writes:

"The architecture field is a small branch of Western culture. It nevertheless extends all over the developed world with outposts even in remotely non-Western societies. That is not to say that it represents the only architectural tradition. China, Japan, India, the Middle east, Africa, and the Pre-Columbian America all have rich architectural histories stretching back to ancient times. But it is the *Western tradition that has ridden the expansive wave of twentieth- and twenty-first-century globalization*, and for that reason the examples used in this book are mostly drawn from that tradition. Often, the examples might as easily have been chosen from non-Western traditions; in the few cases they have [been]. But in other cases, such as [in the] discussion of harmonic proportions, only Western examples will do. Some might see this as an annoying inconsistency, but this is a practical as well as a theoretical book. *It does not aim to break new ground but to be a guide for newcomers to a territory already mapped out, and that territory, like history itself, is partial, biased, and heterogeneous.*"[9] (emphasis added)

Why has only Western tradition "*ridden the expansive wave*"? Should globalization alone be the indicator for architectural literature or is there a place for architectural diversity within education?

My own experience of teaching and writing about Indian vernacular architecture made me realize how casually it is treated by Western academe. An example would be when I was revising my chapters on Indian architecture and art for the 20th anniversary edition of the *Encyclopedia of Vernacular Architecture of the World* (Bloomsbury, second edition, 2023). I realized that the questions being asked by the editors were due to a lack of basic knowledge; they were all based in Europe and the US. I asked the commissioning editor why my editors were from a Western background with no specialist knowledge of Indian architecture, and more so, with none of them ever having visited India. "Why didn't you try to find some Indian academics to edit?" I enquired. The editor responded, "[The Professor] is a highly respected world authority on Chinese vernacular architecture, with much fieldwork experience in the region, and had edited works on Asian vernacular before, so from my perspective he was the right choice."

That a professor and the editor of a major publication could equate knowledge about Chinese vernacular architecture with that of Indian was indeed perplexing. It appears that some attitudes have never changed—James Mill, the Scottish historian who wrote the three-volume *The History of British India*, and who was the most influential colonial historian of India (and the father of the philosopher and activist, John Stuart Mill) never learnt any Indian language nor had he visited India. This reminds me of a recent obituary of a British architect and educator, where he was written about as "a progressive left-wing thinker, ardently anti-violence, anti-colonialist, and committed to education and teaching [and a feminist] but yet he only referenced Western thinkers such as Grosz, Fluxus, Beuys, the Venturis, Foucault and Deleuze."[10]

2. The Continuation of Historic Reasons for the Lack of Indian Architectural Literature

There have been visitors and travelers—right back to ancient times—when Africans and Europeans began to visit Asia, traveling on the Silk Road or via the sea. In India, the Silk Road had its inroads into seven modern states in India: Bihar, Jammu and Kashmir, Punjab, Uttar Pradesh (North), Maharashtra (west), and Puducherry and Tamil Nadu (South). The trade between African and European nations via the sea also constituted an important part of the cultural exchange that led to the development in architecture and art on both sides. Therefore, it is not through the lack of knowledge about India and Asia where this lack of understanding of Indian art begins. Rather, it might be a complex situation involving factors such as colonization and cultural subjugation, exoticization, and a lack of understanding of the Indian view of art and architecture.

The appropriation and hold over the knowledge of Indian architecture continues in a neo-colonial fashion, with grants, scholarships, and awards tightly controlled and curated by Western intentions, structures, and funding. Even Indian academics who are invited to speak and write are those who are supervised, curated, or chosen by Western academics. Further, within academic culture, visiting "exotic" places, such as India, and gathering a limited idea of Indian architecture in as little as ten days without any prior reading,[11] and designing in that context is encouraged, even engaged by many academic institutions. Such academic musings do little to help dispel the trope of the helpless or witless Indians, waiting to be informed by their superiors on what action to take or even what to notice. Further, the very cause of many problems manifested in India—such as the climate and environmental crises—in which the West plays a leading part are not explored in such romantic visions and narratives. India remains in the beholder's eyes, not thoughts.

2.1 Mythical Thinking: Western "Tradition" and Architectural Literature

What has been described in section 1.3 as the "Western tradition" is a temporal condition. Traditional architecture in any region has varied from time to time, as has the concept of vernacular tradition.[12] So has Western architecture varied from time to time. However, the issue that Davies insinuates, or even assumes, earlier on is that Western architecture has advanced in time while non-Western architecture has stood still. Hence he concluded that Western architecture has been a bigger influence than non-Western architecture. The examples of non-Western architecture he referenced previously are actually centuries old: the Ise Shrine in Japan (4 BCE), the Dravidian Hindu temples of Southern India (11–12 CE) and the vernacular architecture of Morocco (which is too diverse to be defined precisely in time)—none are modern examples. Davies further says that in the discussion about harmonic principles that "only Western examples will do." However, harmonic principles were enunciated by the Indian mathematician Acharya Pingala in 4th BCE, long before the Italian, Leonardo Fibonacci (or Bonacci), in 11th CE. Indian architecture, particularly temple spires, display such harmonic proportions. It is to be noted that Fibonacci's father was an Italian merchant and customs official based in Bugia (Béjaïa) in modern-day Algeria, the capital of the Hammadid empire. Fibonacci came across the Indian numeric system during his education in Algeria. It is very likely that his theory developed from the Hindu-Arabic mathematical system he encountered as in his *Liber Abaci* (1202), he introduced the so-called modus Indorum (method of the Indians). However, this is not normally acknowledged in Western academe, as the quote proves.

2.2 Curating and Categorizing Indian Architecture

Amartya Sen, the Indian economist and Nobel Laureate, has defined three different approaches to understanding and interpreting Indian traditions: exoticist, magisterial, and curatorial.[13] Palestinian American thinker, Edward Said has written much about the exoticizing of the Near East and we can extend the East to include India (as he does in his book, *Orientalism*, 1978, with frequent references to India). In Said's view, "the limitations of Orientalism are the limitations that follow upon disregarding, essentializing, [and] denuding the humanity of another culture, people, or geographical region. But orientalism has taken a further step than that: it views the Orient as something whose existence is not only displayed, but has remained fixed in time and place for the West."[14] In other words, the Orient is seen as a backdrop to the modernity of the Occident.

The categorization of Indian architecture was always going to be difficult. The diversity of indigenous Indian architecture was not easy to manage, regulate, and direct for colonial life, especially from thousands of miles away. As the architectural historian and author Jan Morris points out, the "British never homogenized India,"[15] but equally, they could never have, as the economist Amartya Sen likes to point out. Instead, they embarked on standardization and supplanting of the native architecture with imported ones,[16] justifying this with racial overtones, primitiveness, or exoticness of Indian architecture. Even when elements from Indian and Asian cultures, such as pacifism, vegetarianism, Hinduism, and Zoroastrianism were incorporated into the Bauhaus movement, Johannes Itten, the Swiss artist, declared: "Visual art (painting, sculpture, [and] architecture), the art of tones, and of the word, comes to full fruition only in the white race."[17] (Figure 2)

2.2.1 Exoticization, Appropriation, and the Interpretation of Indian Architecture

The "special qualities of Asian art"[18] were never explored properly in colonized countries such as India. Instead, its art and architecture were appropriated, interpreted, and compared using Western standards, and offered for uncritical inspection in the days when people did not travel much. This was achieved through exhibitions like the Great Exhibition in London (1851) or quicky follies like the surrealist Palais Ideal in France (1878). But even the surrealists saw

Figure 2
The context is always important in the appreciation of architecture: the *jaali* screen on the left is from Humayun's Tomb, a World Heritage site in New Delhi, India, and the *jaali* screen on the right is found at Victoria and Albert Museum, London, United Kingdom. The fine stone carving is apparent in both; the in-situ screen (left) is animated by sunlight and shadows and speaks of climate, context, and materiality.

"ethnographic artefacts [from non-Western sources]" as "the epitome" because they seemed to refer to a mythical world beyond visible reality"[19]—in other words, the exoticization of the unknown. Not only was the examination of Indian architecture and culture a pastime of rich colonizers with more time on their hands than qualifications, but the curation of Indian architecture was dependent upon the British historian who patronized a particular style or building, or even a particular place.[20]

The other way of interpreting Indian traditions was "magisterial,"—in other words, through colonial eyes, for example, Thomas Babbington Macaulay's interpretation of Indian culture.[21] This interpretation demotes Indian architecture to being exotic, inferior, and irrelevant to the modern discourse on architecture. Instead, for inspiration and interest, the British looked toward America, a settler colonial country, not India. Roger Dixon and Stefan Muthesius, in their book *Victorian Architecture* state, "Most Englishmen travelled, and even left traces of their architecture in [the many] Victorian cities throughout the Empire: one of the most splendid of all railway stations is that of Bombay, designed in 1878 by F. W. Stevens. But they found little to interest them in the contemporary architectural production of other countries. The *relationship with the United States was different*."[22] (emphasis added) This thread of history continues to be woven into the present, where debates and discussions about Indian architecture are not to be found within the UK's academe, while Western countries such as the US are in the discourse.

2.3 Modern Movement, Education, and Building Standards

Another reason for ignoring Indian architecture in Western education is the assumption that Western tradition is "modern" and progressive and that of Asian countries is not. But as the 20th CE Japanese philosopher and folk craft pioneer, Soetsu Yanagi questioned, "Why does everything 'modern' have to be seen through Western eyes?"[23] Because of such notions, the technical expertise of Indian architecture was not respected. The stone masons who carved the majestic cave temples of India and the structural work in Hindu and Islamic architecture and the fine carvings are not given adequate credit. The material composition of the Iron Pillar from the 4th CE Gupta Empire, which has not rusted despite being exposed to centuries of vagrant weather has not been uncovered, even by NASA scientists; the trabeated arches of India are called "false arches" in Western history books despite their technical sophistication. However, there has been a small win. The stone carving techniques that were passed on through the centuries were finally put into full use when BAPS Shri Swaminarayan Mandir was completed in London in 1995 by specialist stone carvers and masons flown in from India.

So strong has been the colonial influence that it has undermined critical architectural discourse in India. Amartya Sen says that the colonial experience of India has not only undermined the intellectual self-confidence of Indians, but has also been hard on the type of recognition that Indians may themselves have standardly given to the country's scientific and critical discussions.[24] India still uses the modified forms of British standards from colonial times, eschewing its own heritage. The reference to Indian vernacular materials, such as earth, straw, and bamboo, as weak/temporary materials or kutcha, and brick and concrete as modern pukka materials further reinforced the inferiority of Indian traditional materials. Indeed, Indian words such as pukka, veranda, and bungalow have entered the English lexicon. Later, large-scale brick making technology, such as the Bull's Trench kiln, and the use of concrete would wreak havoc on the Indian environment by causing pollution and soil destruction, and replace traditional building skills and materials, such as traditional bricks, mortar (*surkhi*), and lime-based plaster.

2.4 The Bias in Collection and Documentation

Do colonial biases have a responsibility toward the collections of architecture literature that we have today? Author Jan Morris explains that "the fundamental purpose of British imperialism was commercial; the pursuit of 'profit,' not [the] betterment of the people and the land they conquered."[25] During British rule, institutions such as the Schools of Oriental and African Studies (SOAS) and centers for studies of South Asian art in various Oxbridge colleges were established, but ironically, there were no such comparative institutions in India. The reason was simply that such studies were instruments for strengthening Britain's political, commercial, and military presence in Asia and Africa—its very function was to train people in imperialism,[26] not to further the arts. Thus, very little was done to encourage Indians to document their own culture, while much was done to appropriate that culture for exoticization. Today, there are indologists, sinologists, and experts on every Asian country in the West (also in the East), but not such reciprocal experts in Asia on Western architecture.

While authors such as Percy Brown (Indian), George Mitchell (Islamic), Jan Morris (Colonial), and David McCutcheon (Bengali) have created their own legacy, they do not appear to have made a mark on global architectural history the way E. H. Gombrich and Nikolaus Pevsner have for Western art and architecture. Even the work of the British Indian architect, Laurie Baker, has been exoticized as it was created in India, even though such buildings could have been constructed in Britain. The use of colonial era textbooks and standards and a building industry prone to corruption and workers with illiteracy have resulted in tragic collapses, design faults, and resource depletion in the Indian subcontinent. Yet, it has not resulted in buildings of better quality—whether in construction or design. Neither has it become a critical discourse on the nature of building construction in schools of architecture or within architectural journals either in the UK or India.

2.4.1 Appreciation of the Differences

Partha Mitter points out, the "interesting question is not what Indian art shares with Western art, but how it differs from it."[27] The Western ideal of simplicity, taken to its most severe form in modern architecture, failed to appreciate the "ornamentation of Hindu temples as an essential expression of its taste,"[28] despite its own cathedrals and castles which were highly decorated. There was failure by British art historians to understand and accept the anonymity of authorship[29] (many Indian architectural structures are not attributable to individual architects), plurality, syncretic dimensions, assimilation, and diversity—features also commonly found in many Asian cultures and architecture. For example, consider the Hindu and Buddhist architecture of India, which is so different from that found in Thailand, Bali, China, and Japan, yet both come from a common religious basis. Examining the classical and formal traditions of architecture in Asia, we can see that the informal or vernacular traditions have suffered an even worse fall from grace of academe. The reduction of the vernacular architecture of most countries to "primitivism," or as architecture without "architects"—as in the title of the eponymous book—conveys a sense of leaving behind the past and moving into a progressive future. Yet, millions continue to live in such hand-built, vernacular structures all over the world, including Asia.[30]

2.4.2 The Appreciation of Commonalities

Yet, we find that modernist architecture has not escaped the touch of Oriental art forms. The art deco and art nouveau movements have been influenced by Japan, China, India, and other parts of the world. The 19th CE buildings of Brighton (the Royal Pavilion and tea rooms), Sezincote in the UK, and outposts of the British Empire in Kuala Lumpur, Singapore, and Sri Lanka all display the influence of "Indo-Saracenic" forms. In turn, the architecture of India and other Asian countries also have eclectic sources of inspiration from the West to the East. These include the modern brutalist buildings of Raj Rewal and B. V. Doshi, the Empiricist Lotus Temple in New Delhi, India, by Iranian architect Fariborz Sahba, which was constructed by a multinational group of companies, and the India International Center (also in Delhi) by Stein, Doshi & Bhalla, along with a host of revivalist buildings combining Indian and Western architectural forms by architects of the Empire, such as Edwin Lutyens and Herbert Baker, followed by works of Indian architects like Ashoka Hotel and various government buildings in New Delhi and other cities.

The point is, differentiating, deconstructing, and categorizing Eastern and Western traditions is a complex task. It also points to an area of research that will normalize studying Indian architecture in the UK and contribute significantly to diversity in teaching and research. In the meanwhile, we find that the digital world has evolved differently, and perhaps, more inclusively and equitably. Digital sources may hold the key to offset the lack of Indian architecture in the academe of the UK.

3. Conclusion

3.1 The Significance of the Digitization of Architectural Literature

Online architecture publications such as Dezeen, ArchDaily, Architizer, ArchiNet, Rethinking the Future (RTF, which was founded by an Indian architect), and many others have shed light on non-Western architecture and architects. Out of these, Dezeen and Architizer do more than others in having contributions and discussions about non-Western architecture (Dezeen's third largest readership comes from India). Dezeen is the world's most popular and influential architecture, interior, and design magazine, with three million monthly readers and seven million social media followers. Whether they decided to have more content about Indian architects, and thereby, attracted the Indian audience, or it was the other way round, does not matter. Recently, the magazine ran an article about Indian architects' favorite buildings—though not all architects selected Indian buildings, it nevertheless gave an audience to both architects and the buildings.

3.1.2 Access to Digital Architectural Literature and Writings

The significance of these emerging online publications is that they are freely available and accessible on smart phones and tablets; that is they can be viewed anywhere and from any geographical location. For example, RTF says that it was founded due to the need for a "platform that encourages and promotes excellence in architecture on a global scale" and says that it "provides global exposure and opportunities for constructive criticism and an online library of knowledge and inspiration just a click away." It even provides online courses in architecture. For the global audience of architecture students and practitioners, this omnipresence is a great attraction, especially for a young, English-speaking and digitally engaged country like India. These online publications also offer continent and country-specific competitions and products, hence their popularity is understandable as they sometimes also double as a publicity platform for the country's architects and architecture. Another way that architecture continues to shape the environment, values, and intellect of millions is through its literature—both printed and online.

3.1.3 Secondary Sources of Indian Architectural Literature and Influence

Exhibitions, images, installations, artefacts, and prizes can be considered secondary sources of architectural academe as they help to promote, educate, and facilitate debates on critical issues within architecture. Even auction houses such as Christie's and Sotheby's, and museums, such as Victoria and Albert Museum and the British Museum can offer such contextual education. Contemporary architecture from the Indian subcontinent—such as Krushi Bhawan, a government building in Odisha designed by Lotus Studio, which features an elaborate brick façade that helps with passive cooling; the community hospital in Bangladesh designed by Kashef Chowdhury of URBANA, which was the winner of the 2021 RIBA International Prize; and works by Yasmeen Lari, the Pakistani architect—could feature amongst the works selected for architectural education and discourse. The bestowing of the RIBA Royal Gold Medal to B. V. Doshi in 2022, almost 40 years after awarding it to another Indian, Charles Correa, has also helped to move the discourse about Indian architecture within the academe. Doshi's work and books are being read and discussed online[31] and with it, there has been a renewed understanding of modern Indian architecture, as interpreted by an Indian architect. Yasmeen Lari received the 2023 RIBA Royal Gold Medal with an unorthodox set of works made of vernacular materials such as bamboo, earth, and thatch—almost unthinkable within the Western context. This again illustrates that there is an appetite to examine such contexts within architecture.

3.2 Global Connections and Solutions

Understanding the links between climate crisis, modern buildings, and global energy use is another aspect that could benefit from discursive and critical debates during education, and students have shown a keen appetite for engaging here. According to Jeremy Lent, culture shapes value and values shape history.[32] Chitra Viswanath, an Indian architect working with low energy building materials says, "As an architect, we shape the built environment in ways that affect people's lives. From designing homes where families can create memories to designing public spaces where people can come together and connect with one another, architecture has a profound impact on people's experiences and well-being."[33]

Western architectural culture (or rather its imposition in various forms from globalization, colonization, industrialization, and advertising) has shaped our values, and in turn, those values have shaped the architectural history that we read, understand, and create with. The bias in historic collections and libraries may be due to past historiography, which includes architecture and architects

Figure 3
Ramadan Pavilion—an installation at Victoria and Albert Museum, United Kingdom (UK), created by Shahed Salem, an architect of Indian heritage, bringing to the UK contemporary meaning and form to the understanding of Islamic architecture

who fit the traditional canon (Western and male). According to architectural historian Rachel Lee, "Architectural and planning history continues to be dominated by occidental, masculine narratives that overlook building practices in many parts of the world, and the hagiographic canon of white male architects still casts long shadows across the field."[34] However, things may be changing due to a paradigm shift in understanding global and colonial history. Artefacts are being returned, architecture of non-Western countries have started being taught, documented, and written about, and conferences and seminars are being held on the subject. Simon Allford, former President of RIBA, stated that the selection of Yasmeen Lari for the 2023 RIBA Royal Gold Medal made him reflect on the "*value of skills learnt at architecture school*" and that "[Lari's model] is both a broad and relevant model of reuse and reinvention that *we can learn from.*"[35] (emphasis added)

Righting the historical neglect of indigenous architecture by giving first place to an exotic architecture (usually Western) in academe is more than just rejecting the latter and giving first place to the native. We have come too far to ignore the effect of modern European architecture and it is revisionist to try to impose the past on the future. The sense of place has become ever more important. Marina Tabassum exhorts us "to create appropriate buildings with 'a sense of place',"[36] which is something she believes has been lost as architecture has become more homogenous over the past 30 years. Digitalization, shared discourses on architecture, and the creation of decolonized knowledge base are all useful tools in the creation of an equitable and diverse profession that serves and appreciates all (Figure 3).

Notes

1. In 2012, 10 percent of Indians claimed to speak English. See Zareer Masani, "English or Hinglish—which will India Choose?" *BBC News* online, 27 November, 2012, https://www.bbc.co.uk/news/magazine-20500312.
2. For example, see https://www.firstinarchitecture.co.uk/14-books-every-architecture-student-should-read/.
3. "Ethnicity of the UK Population and the Register," Architects Registration Board, accessed April 12, 2023, https://arb.org.uk/architects-today/?dm_i=4ZCL,T664,1J6G71,3N35Y,1.
4. "India Receives Largest Share of UK Study, Work, and Visit Visas," British High Commission, August 26, 2022, https://www.gov.uk/government/news/india-receives-largest-share-of-uk-study-work-and-visit-visas.
5. http://exhibition.monass.org/, accessed March 6, 2023.
6. AR Editors, "Unit 6 — London Metropolitan University," July 22, 2010, *The Architectural Review*, https://www.architectural-review.com/essays/unit-6-london-metropolitan-university.
7. James Fergusson embarked upon a second career as an architectural historian and categorized Indian architecture from the profits of the plantation and the labors of Indians.
8. Partha Chatterjee, *The Nation and Its fragments* (United States: Princeton University Press, 1993), 6.
9. Colin Davies, *Thinking about Architecture: An Introduction to Architecture* Theory (London, United Kingdom: Laurence King Publishing, 2011), 11.
10. Richard Waite, "Tributes Paid to FAT and London School of Architecture Co-founder Clive Sall," February 23, 2023, *Architect's Journal*, https://www.architectsjournal.co.uk/news/tributes-paid-to-fat-and-london-school-of-architecture-co-founder-clive-sall (accessed 2 March 2023).
11. "Embarking on the first phase of fieldwork, we had a very limited sense of how the monsoon was conceptualised and understood by people."—Monsoon Multiplicities exhibition by Monsoon Assemblages (University of Westminster, United Kingdom), a research project funded by the European Research Council to conduct research on monsoons in Bangladesh, India, London, and Myanmar "as an open-ended gathering of human, non-human, and planetary ways of being and knowing," accessed March 3, 2023, http://exhibition.monass.org/.
12. The Vernacular Architecture Group was formed in 1952 to further the study of traditional buildings, originally those of the British Isles. In recent years, its membership and publications have also reflected a growing interest in buildings from other parts of the world, thus widening its scope.
13. Amartya Sen, *The Argumentative Indian* (United Kingdom: Allen Lane Publishing, 2005), 141.
14. Edward W. Said, *Orientalism*, originally published in 1978 as *Orientalism: Western Conceptions of the Orient* (Penguin, 2003), 108.
15. Jan Morris, *Stones of an Empire* (United Kingdom: Oxford University Press, 1983), 8.
16. While statues and parts of buildings, and gold and jewelry were looted and transported to the UK, it was not possible to do so with entire buildings. And so, with some reluctance perhaps, and with some interest in the exotic, architecture was documented by the colonizers—particularly if these were places of worship as their

destruction could set off more unrest. So, in the buildings of New Delhi from 1907, temples, astronomical structures (Jan Mantar), and mosques were preserved.

17. Johannes, "Itten, Rassenlehre und Kunstentwicklung" [Racial Theory and Art Development], *Madasnan* 16, no. 5 (1923): 89–92.

18. Partha Mitter, *Indian Art* (United Kingdom: Oxford University Press, 2001), 144.

19. Objects of Desire: Surrealism and Design 1924–Today, exhibition, Design Museum, London, October 14, 2022–February 19, 2023.

20. For example, in 1914, author, E. M. Forster was puzzled by the lack of British interest in the ancient city of Ujjain, India, an architectural gem.

21. Thomas Babbington Macaulay intoned that "a single shelf of a good European library was worth the whole native literature of India and Arabia and that [he] certainly never met with any orientalist who ventured to maintain that Arabic and Sanskrit poetry could be compared to that of the great European nations." ("Minute by the Honorable T. B. Macaulay, dated February 2, 1835," accessed March 16, 2023, https://www.cambridge.org/core/books/abs/competition-wallah/education-in-india-since-1835-with-a-minute-of-lord-macaulay/A55D9C24D87D5C71FBA75A9CA57117FC.)

22. Roger Dixon and Stefan Muthesius, *Victorian Architecture* (United Kingdom: Thames and Hudson, 1985), 28.

23. Soetsu Yanagi, *The Beauty of Everyday things* (Penguin Classics, 2018), 143.

24. Amartya Sen, *The Argumentative Indian* (United Kingdom: Allen Lane Publishing, 2005), 77.

25. Jan Morris, *Stones of an Empire*, 2.

26. Regina Bittner and Kathrin Rhomberg, eds., *The Bauhaus in Calcutta: An encounter of Cosmopolitan Avant-Gardes* (Germany: Hatje Cantz, 2013), 79.

27. Partha Mitter, *Indian Art*.

28. ibid, 2.

29. "Without [authorship], architecture would lose its special relationship to history, from which it draws its cultural and critical depth."—Colin Wilson, *Thinking about Architecture: An Introduction to Architectural Theory* (London, United Kingdom: Laurence King Publishing, 2010), 137.

30. In this instance, it is good to reference Paul Oliver's monumental work, *The Encyclopedia of the Vernacular Architecture of the World* (Cambridge University Press, 1997), which presents the extraordinary world of indigenous architecture in all its technical, social, and environmental aspects.

31. "Balakrishna Doshi," *Dezeen*, accessed April 14, 2023, https://www.dezeen.com/tag/balkrishna-doshi/.

32. Jeremy Lent, *Patterning Instinct: A Cultural History of Humanity's Search for Meaning* (United States: Prometheus Books, 2017), 28.

33. Chitra Viswanath, email sent to author, March 6, 2023.

34. Rachel Lee, "Transnational Assemblages," in *AA Women in Architecture 1917–2017*, eds. Lynne Walker and Elizabeth Darling (London, United Kingdom: AA Publications, 2017). The female Thai architect, Korani Surintraboon, appears in *The Architect and Building Design* (April 3, 1963), in a photo with Otto Königsberger, promoting his views about tropical architecture, however, nothing else is known or written about her. According to Rachel Lee, assistant professor of History of Architecture and Urban Planning, Delft University of Technology, The Netherlands, the Architectural Association, "which [was] adept at using the photos of women from former colonies to promote itself as a progressive institution," also erased them after that photo opportunity.

35. Simon Allford, "Lessons for All Life," *RIBA Journal* 130, no. 5 (May 2023): 72.

36. Cajsa Carlson, "'Wherever I work I Must Understand that Place,' says Marina Tabassum," *Dezeen*, March 4, 2022, https://www.dezeen.com/2022/03/04/marina-tabassum-bangladeshi-architect-interview/.

Figure Credits

Table 1: Comparisons of architectural literature available on popular websites and educational institutions of the UK (author's diagram).

Figure 1: Marriage halls in Western style on a road in West Delhi (author's photo).

Figure 2: The context is always important in the appreciation of architecture: *Jaali* screens from Humayun's Tomb (left), a World Heritage Site in New Delhi, India, and Victoria and Albert Museum (right), London, United Kingdom. The fine stone carving is apparent in both (author's photo).

Figure 3: Ramadan Pavilion—an installation at Victoria and Albert Museum, United Kingdom (UK), created by Shahed Salem, an architect of Indian heritage, bringing to the UK contemporary meaning and form to the understanding of Islamic architecture (author's photo).

Writing Architectural Pedagogies

Anuradha CHATTERJEE, School of Design and Innovation, RV University

Anuradha Chatterjee is Pro Vice-Chancellor and Dean, School of Design & Innovation, RV University. She is an Indian-born Australian academic practitioner in architecture and design based in Australia and India. Dr Chatterjee is Regional Editor Asia Pacific, *TEXTILES: Cloth and Culture*; a registered architect at the Council of Architecture, India; an Associate of Australian Institute of Architects; and elected Companion, Guild of St George. She is the author of three books as solo editor, *Surface and Deep Histories* (Cambridge Scholars Publishing); author, *Built, Unbuilt, and Imagined Sydney* (Copal Publishing); author, *John Ruskin and the Fabric of Architecture* (Routledge). She is the Area Editor (Asia) for the fourth publication, *The Bloomsbury Global Encyclopedia of Women in Architecture 1960–2015* (eds Karen Burns and Lori Brown, forthcoming October 2024). Her fifth book is an edited collection titled *Architectures of Ageing in Place* (under contract, Routledge, 2025).

Abstract

This paper is focused on making a case for the importance of literary pedagogies in architecture. The first part delineates the bridges between architecture and literature (in the broad sense) that have emerged historically; and they consist of five unique propositions: architecture and literature, narrative and space, text as spatial practice, impossible feminist spatial futures, and architecture and/as research. Using these five positions, the second part of the paper builds a case for literary emergency in architecture. The third part demonstrates three case studies from my own academic practice that are manifestations of a literary approach to architectural education. The fourth and final part of the paper is a postscript that delineates areas of missed opportunities in architectural curriculum in India, with the paper being a call to action, to return to the origins and foundations of architecture as a literary and intellectual discipline.

Author Information
Anuradha CHATTERJEE: architecturalhistorytheory@gmail.com

Keywords

Literary, pedagogy, literature, writing.

1. Introduction

The connection between language and architecture is a historically and epistemologically complex and contested terrain, but we negotiate and navigate it with agreements and disagreements. While language and architecture are inextricably linked, architecture can be said to have its own language in the same way that literature can be said to have its own architecture. Further, there is an enormous body of significant literary work around buildings, architects, and cities, in terms of theories, histories, analyses, and criticisms. Yet, here is another paper on writing and architecture with a focus on pedagogy. One might ask: What is the aim? The fact is, the case still needs to be made, or re-made, on the significance of writing in architectural education, which has diminished steadily, with the link to practice and professional "competency" further eroded.

For the purposes of this paper, the inquiries will focus on the liminal boundary between the written word and the built world, and the overlaps as well as slipperiness between the two, structuring the paper into four parts. The first part will delineate the bridges between architecture and literature—in the broad sense but avoiding discussions of writing about architecture and writing in architecture, which survive and thrive, but to varying degrees of success. The second part will make a case on literary pedagogies. In the third part, three pedagogical approaches (teaching projects) are presented, from my own transnational academic practice, not just to demonstrate methodologies for engaging literature in architectural education as an academic exercise, but to also suggest the possibility that these are forms of experimental architectural practice. The fourth and final part of the paper is a postscript, which identifies missed opportunities and suggests the way forward for a more evolved architectural curriculum.

2. Of Architectural Disciplinarities

2.1 Literature and Architecture

The first proposition is about the compelling ways in which architecture and literature come together in articulating modernity. David Spurr's *Architecture and Modern Literature* is a significant book which explores this theme, through a study of writings that "appear to break down the barriers between the two art forms, or at least to construct bridges between [them]."[1] Architecture was important because it was used by many writers to foreground anxieties, alienation, and dysfunctionalities around the crisis of meaning and inhabiting the modern world. Spurr reminds us of the "basic truth that the human world is literally structured as the built environment, and symbolically structured as language. The art of the built environment is architecture; that of language is literature. Herein is reason enough to consider their common ground."[2] For the purposes of this paper, I will bring focus to writers like Franz Kafka, Gaston Bachelard, and Georges Perec—also covered in Spurr's book—as I have always been struck by the materiality of interiors and other spaces and built forms in their writings.

According to Spurr, Kafka, writing in the early twentieth century, often "described his own writing in architectural terms," referring to it "as a process of construction (*aufbauen*), but in a way that also makes this a construction of the self."[3] Spurr adds that there is an

> intimacy between "writing and the self," almost as if "through the constructive process of writing, could Kafka himself come into being, not just as a writer but as a human being."[4]

Roger N. Thiel, similarly, notes Kafka's observations (in his diary), where he writes: "Everything appears to me to be an artificial construction," and "I am on the hunt for constructions."[5] Thiel also notes that Kafka's novels are full of all kinds of architectural forms and structures, which often serve as "organizing principles and poetological devices: cities, squares, palaces, cathedrals; walls, towers, pits; staircases, stairs, windows, doors, gates, attics, roofs; galleries, bridges, streets." However, he also notes that they are not deployed to applaud the positive qualities of these structures—these are not enduring structures. They cannot defend or protect and they are bound to fail or be destroyed. In trying to depict the condition of spiritual homelessness, Kafka's "towers cannot be built, bridges give way, and buildings cannot provide shelter."[6] His constructions and deconstructions speak to the societal condition of living in "dysfunctional communities characterized by failed communication," and the "instabilities and dislocations" they embody, which are otherwise suppressed.[7]

Peta Mitchell argues that by the time Georges Perec was writing, the connection between architecture and literature—especially the post-structuralist theorization of buildings as texts—was starting to gain ground (via Peter Eisenmann and Jacques Derrida).[8] Novels in which architecture was not just a backdrop but the "stage upon which everyday social life could be enacted" characterized French literature since before France's second empire.[9] However, argues Mitchell, Perec's *La Vie mode d'emploi* [Life: a User's Manual] (1978), set in a fictitious block of flats in the Rue Simon-Crubellier in Paris, France, does so much more than represent the literature of his time: he "fuses his interests in the everyday and architecture into what might be termed an "architext," whereby the "book and building become one."[10] One cannot say *Life: a User's Manual* is set in an apartment building. It is written in a way such that the "book is the apartment building itself."[11] Premised on recovering the quotidian and the everyday, argues Mitchell, Perec creates a "play in the narrative sequencing of the novel's chapter-rooms," inviting the reader to become a participant in unraveling the puzzle that has been constructed.[12]

2.2 Narrative and Space

The second proposition is about narrative in/and architecture. Bernard Tschumi and Nigel Coates's collaboration at London's Architecture Association (AA) in the 70s and 80s, as argued by Claire Jamieson and Rebecca Roberts-Hughes, was influential in shaping these ideas further, but over time, their methodologies also evolved in different directions. Jamieson and Roberts-Hughes note Tschumi's powerful statement in his "Space and Events " (1983) essay, which connects the "unfolding of events in a literary context" to the "unfolding of events in architecture."[13] To this end, Tschumi's approach was to take the "literary text as a resource from which to select narrative sequences that could be projected onto a physical site as the basis for the design of architectural space."[14] It was "deliberate and precise," argue Jamieson and Roberts-Hughes, and related to the "the manipulation of words in a text."[15] In contrast, Coates was more interested in the "effect created by the literary text—sensation, immersion, narrativity—as qualities to be produced by architecture."[16] In essence, while Tschumi was trying to "create new forms," Coates was seeking to "create new narratives constructed through experience."[17]

Sophia Psarra's *Architecture and Narrative* (2009) further unpacks these ideas as she characterizes architecture as a carrier of "content" through the "arrangement of spaces, materials, social relationships, and the cultural purposes."[18] It is linked with "sequence, space, and time," but it is also about structuring and arranging the different parts to make the whole. It is not about the story or the content, rather, it is about the content being structured and presented to an "audience by an authorial entity."[19] Psarra's inquiry is focused on the "relationship between narrative structure, perceptual experience and representation." She adds further that buildings do not just express meanings, but that they are also active in the construction of meanings. What is at stake is not just the conceptual realm of ideas ("patterns we can hold in our mind"), but also the way this is aligned or reconciled with the perceptual realm ("those we grasp gradually through movement") of an embodied experience of visitors.[20] These two realms are not "mutually exclusive;" in fact, they are "different and interacting systems of ordering experience."[21]

2.3 Text as Spatial Practice

The third proposition is about writing as architectural practice.[22] Jane Rendell's articulation of this framing is particularly useful, as she says: "I wish to draw attention to the architectural aspects of the practice of writing, a practice which, like architecture, is both spatial and material, and with which historians, theorists, critics, and designers all engage, and yet [which] is usually rendered invisible."[23] Indeed, writing is an act that is material, spatial, tectonic, and inhabitable. To write is to build, and to read is to inhabit. And while the structuralists' claim that buildings and cities are texts that can be read, it is also possible to imagine texts as architecture. Because, when we read texts, we also simultaneously envision depth, surface, thickness, layers, structure, foundations, and sequence. And when we are speaking about writing, we are also "constructing" an argument, "assembling" evidence, or using a theoretical "scaffold" or "framework." Language and text are always textured and spatial, and writing as a practice of architecture is not a "flat" representation of what is otherwise experienced as built space.

Irish architect and writer Anne Ryan echoes Rendell's frustrations around the marginalization of writing as architecture as she also resonates Jennifer Bloomer's approach to constructive writing: "My writing practice follows the very same motivations. I manipulate words to express an idea. Selecting brick as the sole material with which to define the thresholds, direct the light, texture the ground, sculpt the courtyards, and vault the ceilings of, for example, a domestic house; pushing the use of brick to its very limits operates in an analogous way to shifting word order, varying sentence length, developing fluid yet coherent movement between paragraphs, and intensifying vocabulary. One practice constructs and manipulates three-dimensional space. One practice constructs and manipulates one-dimensional words. But both volumetric enclosure and written text can work through and define spatial ideas. What links both processes of spatial understanding is the person (author-architect) and their negotiation of their surroundings."[24]

Ryan says that if "architecture is a way of thinking about the world," then "making physical buildings" is the most "obvious and most accepted mode of practicing architecture." She asks why it is hard to imagine other ways of practicing, such as "writing architecture" or "writing as architecture," and whether this might be because writing has not been considered as a "mode of representation within the process of constructing architecture."[25]

Figure 1
Naman Pandey, *Glancing through History*, published September 13, 2020

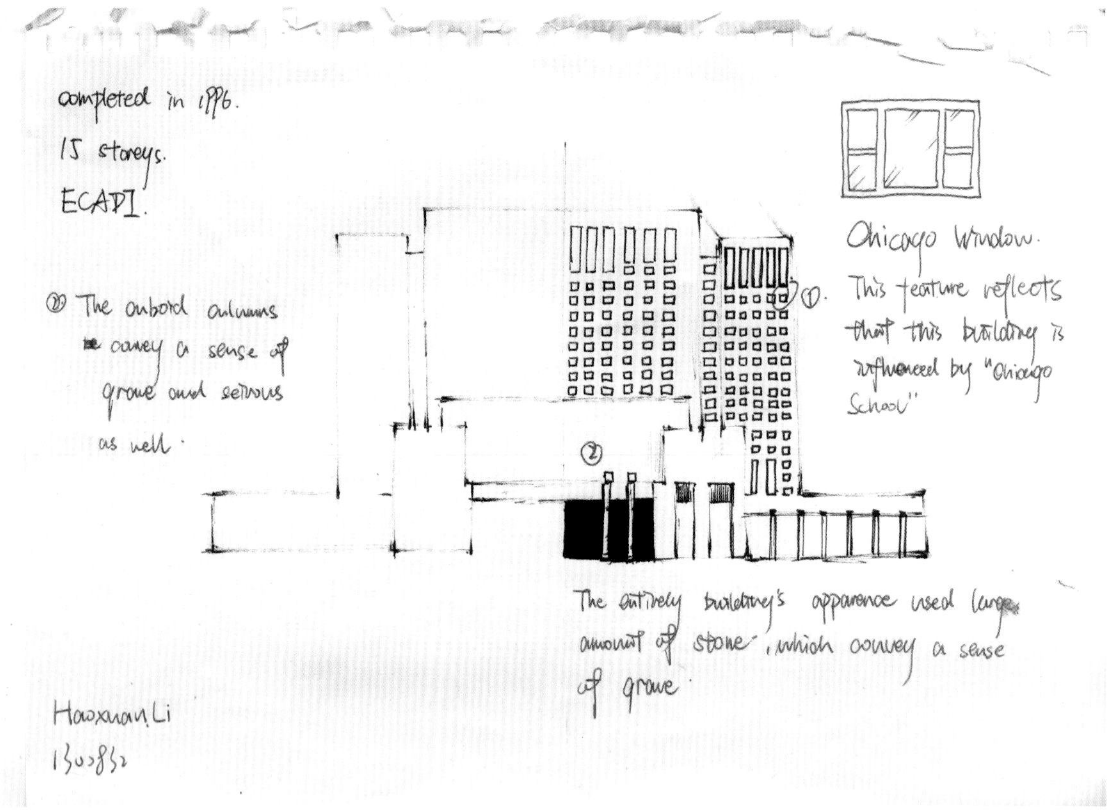

Figure 2
Shanghai field trip drawing 1, Haoxuan Li, 2014; submitted to Xi'an Jiaotong Liverpool University

To this end, while Rem Koolhaas proposed a parallel practice of writing—wherein he explained that all their best or original projects were "first defined in literary terms,"—writers like Italo Calvino offered yet another model of writing as architectural practice—through *Invisible Cities*—which contains "unseen possibilities embedded within the ruins of the city." In John Hejduk's theoretical projects, the writing not only completed the projects but also testified to a "new way of writing."[26]

2.4 Impossible (Feminist) Spatial Futures

The fourth proposition is about spatial futures and fiction. Not only has fiction the pre-emptive power to herald architectural, technological, and spatial futures, but it has also had a strong role to play in holding within it and keeping safe new, subversive, dissonant futures, specifically utopian fiction, including feminist utopian fiction.[27] Jennifer Sue Boyers emphasizes the political significance of feminist utopian fiction as a "medium which allows one to simultaneously critique existing hegemonic power relations and create alternative subversive visions."[28] Examples of this are Rokeya Sakhawat Hossain's *Sultana's Dream* (1905), which is characterized as "one of the earliest science fiction stories written by a woman" and Charlotte Perkins Gilman's *Herland* (1915), which is characterized as a "scientific utopia" and a feminist utopia.[29] The commonality between these two works becomes apparent when one considers how *Sultana's Dream* "shares with *Herland* a playful depiction of a "good society" run by an all-female community harnessed by technology, that is living in peace, sharing, sustainability, and solidarity.[30]

Léone Drapeaud's "Founding the Feminist Utopia" (2018) essay presents a survey of feminist science fiction to suggest the archetypes of city planning that can be utilized for imagining new feminist urban utopias, because architectural history does not really offer alternative spatial/social imaginaries. The archetypes are the fortress, which "creates a new context through isolation," the city as a machine, which seeks to challenge how work is structured so that the "social status of women can be challenged and improved," and the overlay, which is when "existing spaces are subverted, transformed, and questioned, often to the point where pre-existing spaces are barely legible."[31] The archetypes are not intended as instrumental typologies, rather, they are tools that allow us to think of ideal societies, social changes, and how that might be coded into spatial structures. However, most of all, Drapeaud emphasizes—through Erin McKenna—that one cannot let go of utopian thinking as that is like "forfeiting one's future."[32] Literary works are particularly powerful as they contain narratives that have unimaginable spatial (built and unbuilt) consequences.

2.5 Architecture and/as Research

Finally, the fifth proposition about architecture and literature is about the definition of what constitutes research in architecture, even though not all research in architecture is literary. And while not all research in architecture is literary—as a lot of it is through practice and experimental methods, drawing, modeling, making objects, and such— it is a "systematic inquiry directed toward the creation of knowledge," as Linda Groat and David Wang outline through James Snyder.[33] And often, but not always, this is documented and communicated through writing, in combination with other media and publication. There has been a lot of interest in the field of architectural research in the past 10 years, and the interest has been in defining what it is, notwithstanding that the

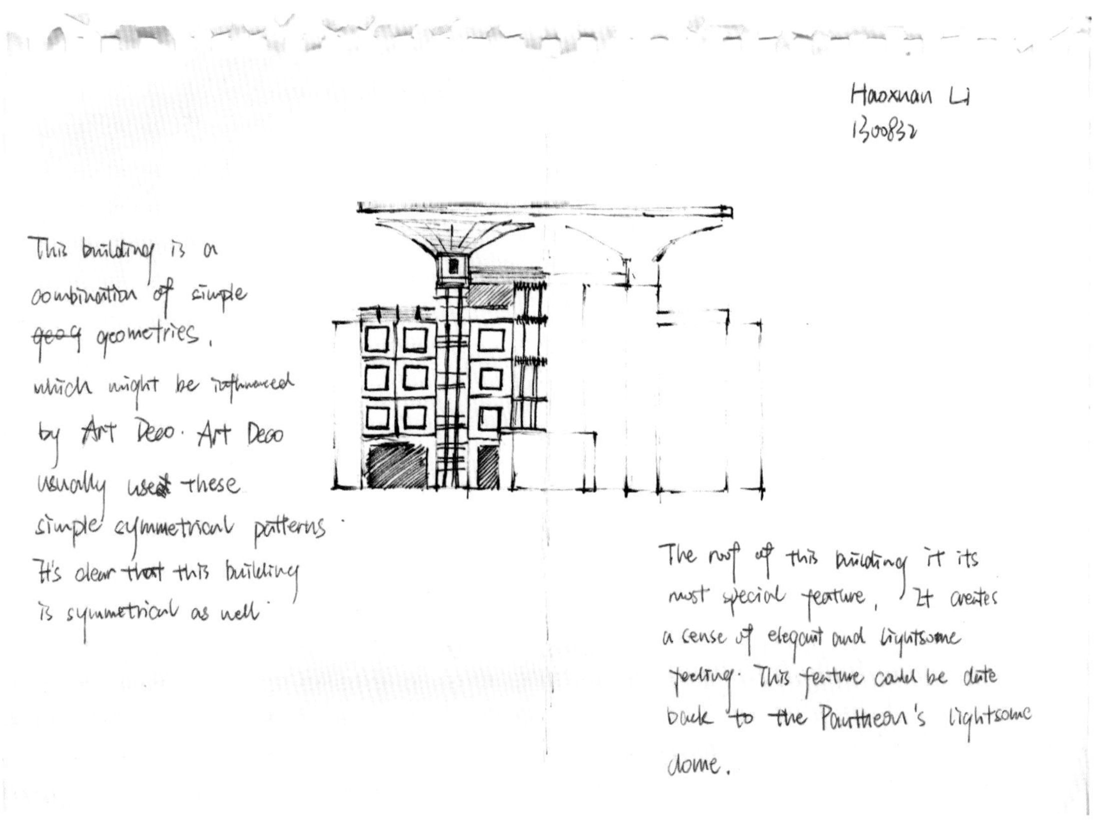

Figure 3
Shanghai field trip drawing 2, Haoxuan Li, 2014; submitted to Xi'an Jiaotong Liverpool University

well-established scholarship in the field of design research (Nigel Cross and Christopher Frayling, for instance) includes architecture and other forms of spatial practice, but is not limited to them.

There are three different ways in which research in architecture might take place across the following three domains of activity, and whilst they can be conceived as stand-alone, they are also often co-informing and intricately imbricated. The first is "Design/Practice as Research," which is "design work with a particular focus on the creation of new insight and knowledge," with a specific focus on the contestation of methodologies and emphasis on speculation, risk, and experimentation.[34] The second is "Research Led Practice," whereby the design process is cognizant of, as well as engaged with, the "state of art" in architectural design scholarship and is also open to engaging with disciplinary knowledge from "outside" architecture. Third is "Practice Based Research" that engages circular processes of testing and/or evaluating performance, making sense of and/or theorizing, undertaking critical interrogations of practice, processes, and buildings, and remaking as appropriate.

3. Of Pedagogies

3.1 Home Grown

It is important for me to note for our readers that these propositions and positions are not a Western import, emerging out of a European and North American discourse. Writing architecture has been a part of the Indian discourse for decades, starting with Gautam Bhatia's extensive "body of unbuilt work encompassing his artworks, writings, and biting satire [which] have provided an accessible platform for both architects and non-architects to reflect on the complexities and attendant absurdities of Indian architecture in its social, economic, and political context," and Busride Design Studio's recent manifestoes of contextual utopias,[35] as well as Rupali Gupte and Prasad Shetty's myriad of speculative essays on the Mumbai public and their *First Questions* book by the School of Environment and Architecture (SEA) Mumbai; Kaiwan Mehta's essays within his editorship of *Domus* and outside of it—all of which is further augmented by Rajesh Advani's edited collections, *Unbuilt 1.0* (2019) and *Unbuilt 2.0* (2022); all these have created even more space for the genre of the architectural essay and critical and speculative writing in India.

3.2 Literary Emergency

As discussed in the previous section, there are many points of intersections between architecture and language—as writing, text, literature, theory, research, narrative, and fiction—and pedagogies in architecture may well take up one or some of these. However, it seems like we are almost always still making a case for writing, literature, and research in architectural education, not because they are so common, but precisely because they are not. As someone who works across professional and academic practice, I see a growing chasm and a disconnect in the industry from the act of writing, research, theory, and language in general in India as well as in Australia. Experienced architects, as well as graduates of architecture, are caught up in the never-ending cycle of making and perfecting drawings, understandably so because there is a crisis—reported formally by academic committees, and more anecdotally by architects—in the field of professional design documentation. To this end, writing in architecture is seen as a low priority, non-essential affinity and/or skill. Not

Figure 4
Tabletop installation of graphic tiles from M. Mukundan's novel, *On the Banks of the Mayyazhi* by students of Avani Institute of Design, 2019

Figure 5
Studio Instagram (sensing space) showing tectonic explorations by students of Avani Institute of Design, 2019

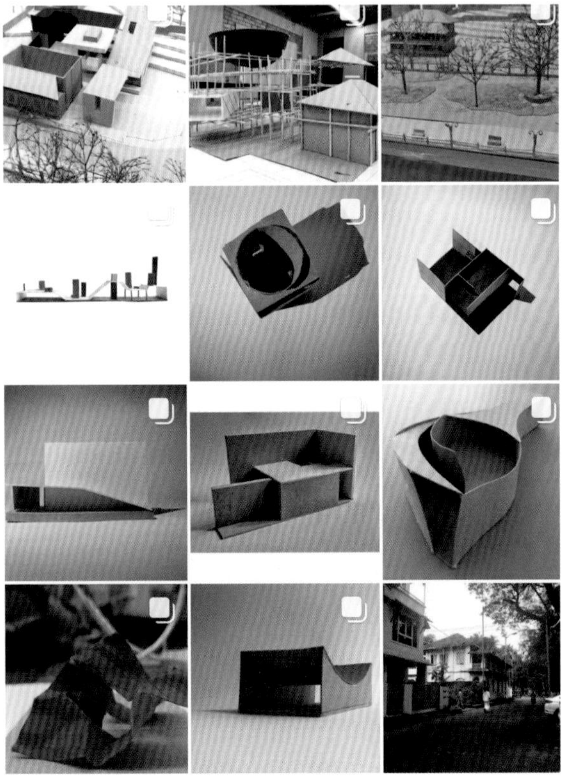

only is this short-sighted because it centers professional competence entirely upon industry needs, but it is also focused on a short-term goal without considering how architects, emerging architects, and graduates might ever engage in a critical, reflexive practice without a recourse to writing. If we were to call for a "literary emergency" in architecture, now would be a good time, for two reasons.

One, research—and with it writing—is urgently needed for the industry and businesses, and even though this seems like a new idea in architecture, it has been "central to the history of the architect for over 500 years."[36] The "business case" for research in contemporary practice is made well by Flora Samuel and Anne Dye who argue that practices are "using research to give clients evidence—as we all know how clients tend to like evidence—about why design makes a difference and on how the practice is continually improving what they do."[37] Hensel and Nilsson contend that notwithstanding the orientation toward branding, business, and competitive benefits that this might deliver, there are "several practices internationally grounded in serious research efforts and collaborations using research to mainly develop the internal culture of the practice, with the open sharing of new knowledge externally."[38] Katharine Martindale adds to this as she argues that practices engage in research to "expand and demonstrate practice expertise," "innovate," "fulfil passion projects," "introduce new thinking," "raise the practice profile," "deliver commissioned research," and to "attract talent."[39] These ideas are bolstered even more in the figure of the *Hybrid Practitioner* (2022), the architect who writes and who simultaneously occupies the critical space between embodied knowledge (in practice) and academic research.[40]

Two, and more importantly, is the centrality of writing in architectural criticism, and therefore, critical practice. Andrew Clancy's *Architectural Review* essay revisits this as he asks: "How can a practice be critical when it is so inherently intertwined with the culture it fundamentally serves? Ours is a time where the agency of the architect has to be developed in negotiation, as a catalyst, or even as an activist."[41] It can be argued that to develop and sustain critical practice, we need to be able to delineate new theories, imagine impossible futures, and articulate radical transformations that are interested in "relentlessly shaking disciplinary foundations, disturbing assumptions rather than reinforcing and disseminating them.[42] Writing and practice, while they move at differential paces and intensities, have the capacity of being complementary discourses, and instead of conforming they challenge and unsettle each other. Critical writing enters architectural discourse in the form of the essay in the eighteenth century, but it needs a more cogent history—a genealogy almost as powerful as the history of architecture as a discursive form.[43] In fact, as criticism is born out of the need to resist conservatism and absolutism, it may be that writing can imagine that which design is hesitant to think and do. Keeping these two points in mind, in the following sections, I will try to reflect upon my academic practice and present three case studies as propositions on literary pedagogies.

4. Three Propositions

4.1 Reading Buildings to Construct Texts

The idea of reading theory, reading buildings against theoretical frameworks, and building theories is a fundamentally literary-tectonic process of studying the history of architecture, which I have explored in various settings. First was for the self-paced, field-based online course, "Chaukhat, Darwaza, Jharokha: Public Life of in-between Elements in Historic Architecture," which I developed and mentored for Acedge (an e-learning platform focused on trends in architecture, construction, engineering, and design in South Asia) between 2018 and 2022. Informed by own scholarship on architectural surface, the course provided the theoretical frameworks of surface as order, decorum, and animation; the source of theatrical urbanity, as shared territories, an event, and as urban; and as reflected repositories and the art of dressing well, to understand how threshold elements contribute to shaping life inside and outside the buildings.[44] Students were expected to use these lenses, visit historic buildings in their urban contexts, read threshold elements in historic buildings, and write new theoretical histories. The aim was not to de-historicize these elements, but to move away from relying on an exclusively text-based and classroom-based education in architectural history. Field study was, therefore, central to this, to subtly challenge the hegemony of canonical knowledge and appreciate new insights emerging from the embodying experience of buildings in context. (Figure 1, page 29)

For similar but slightly other reasons, I used a different methodology for teaching the History of Western Architecture module in Xi'an Jiaotong Liverpool University in China, which was in equal measures literary and tectonic. An important learning objective was to foster a sense of agency and independence in first-year students, especially considering Western education's indoctrination of Chinese students into English language and Western histories, which is constrained further by a lecture-based

Figure 6
(Re)thinking and (Re) making the Threshold Studio—montage showing application of conceptual wall to the existing building, University of New South Wales, 2011

format and a large cohort of 180 students. Therefore, a theoretical subject that was largely about reading and writing had to be more than just that. I proposed that instead of providing students with an essay topic or question, they should find one—which they did by combining two topics of their interest from my lectures. They then had to write a theoretical summary around these two topics and use them as lenses to read the buildings they visited during our annual Shanghai field trip. The way students composed their final essays was tectonic in nature. Constructed over time as an assemblage, it involved assembling topics and summaries as building blocks, using these to read buildings and make drawings, and using the drawings in the essay to present an insight. The process was neither neat nor conventional and there was a lot of collaborative "labor" involved in ensuring that there was an even spread of topics across a large student cohort to allow for distinctiveness in the essays. (Figure 2, page 30; Figure 3, page 31)

4.2 Fiction in Design

Design is an interesting way of understanding fiction, and as Hélène Frichot and Naomi Stead claim: "Every architectural proposition is a kind of speculative fiction before it becomes a built fact, just as every written fiction relies on a setting; the construction of a coherent milieu in which a story can take place."[45] But further to that, fiction also has a function in architectural education, which Klaske Havik and Angeliki Sioli explore, as they argue that "imagination being at the very center of the architectural process, stories, and language can bring forward imaginative possibilities that have long been left on the margins of architectural curricula and pedagogical environments."[46] And while architecturally invested texts like those of Kafka might be an interesting prompt for many educators because the "narrative space in Kafka's texts has ambiguous, incomplete, nonfunctional, non-geometric, and unusual peculiarities that allow students to explore and experience space in new ways,"[47] one may not always be lucky to find the kind of opportunism we found in seeking a foothold for our fifth semester studio at Avani Institute of Design, India. As a studio team, we collectively sought to engage with the complexities of the ex-French colonial town of Mahé in South India, which shares much more than a border with the state of Kerala, but which remains distinct due to its unique political history. Currently in a state of much neglect since its decolonization—with its original population having moved out or migrated overseas—it would have been a tough job for students to engage with the oral histories of the place that are now hard to access, and would have left them grappling with the opaqueness of the everyday.

This is where we decided that we were going to inhabit the fictive space of the 1974 novel by M. Mukundan, *Mayyazhippuzhayude Theerangalil* (translated as *On the Banks of the Mayyazhi*, 1999), which is based on the lives of people in Mahé around the time of its liberation from French rule, written by a novelist who was not only born in the city, but who also lived and worked there.[48] As a studio team, we did not want to document more urban-historical morphologies. We wanted a glimpse into the mythical past of the city. Therefore, we collectively inhabited the space of the novel, using it as our gateway into Mahé, as we sought overlaps between the city's geography—as it was described in the novel and the way that the city is now—mapping spaces and places of significance that have persisted, disappeared, or that never existed, or that existed in other forms. As a design method, each student read one chapter from the book, narrated it to the cohort, identified five sets of spaces (with corresponding event and emotion) that they found compelling, and represented that as a series of graphic tiles. These were then subjected to further artifice as they picked out storylines or threads from this larger narrative and translated them into architectonic forms and spaces shaped to hold the stories and memories that gave rise to them. The architectural program of the Cultural Interpretation Centre was then reconciled into these emergent forms and made legible through logical spatial organization, as well as believable, as structurally buildable masses. (Figures 4 and 5, page 32)

4.3 Design as Dissertation

The format of the design dissertation in architecture curricula in India is a missed opportunity to weave in the idea of design and dissertation, as complementary modes of inquiry. Usually, the design dissertation projects proceed in a linear format, with an intense period of research, analysis, and project conceptualization, followed by a semester of design articulation, resolution, and representation. In the many reviews that I have participated in institutions in India—across Manipal University, Jaipur, School of Environment and Architecture, Mumbai, and Kamla Raheja Vidyanidhi Institute for Architecture (KRVIA), Mumbai—the point that has been made collectively by many educators is to consider research as a parallel inquiry that informs the design as a continuous process, which would mean that research does not stop, it continues as parallel activity that transforms the project-in-the-making, with the overall process taking on a non-linear form. Additionally, it has also been suggested that there is another way to proceed, which is to treat the design project as a form of dissertation. In architecture schools, before thesis became synonymous with design project, it was understood as a proposition, and as Koolhaas argued, design is a "demonstration of a thesis or a question or a literary idea."[49] Engaging with design in this manner—like Salomon suggested—means jumping into design as an iterative, risk-taking process that is driven by inquiry and insight and not just by intention and outcome in search of answers for research questions (of the discipline) posed by and through the design project, whereby the outcome is there as a project, but it is secondary to the insight gained through the inquiry. (Figure 6, page 33)

This is demonstrated in my (Re)thinking and (Re)making the Threshold Studio project at the University of New South Wales, Australia, which marked a trajectory from architectural history scholarship to new theoretical lenses for studying contemporary architecture, to a design studio project.[50] Architectural surface was the focus of my PhD research on John Ruskin, which was extended to look at the theories and histories of the architectural surface. In *Surface and Deep Histories: Critiques, and Practices in Art, Architecture and Design*, I proposed five types of surfaces that persist throughout history and which constitute the "building blocks" of all built artefacts—representational surface, surface as an integrated element, surface as an urban event, surface as a transient phenomenon, and surface as a design tool.[51] These surface typologies were used by students in my University of New South Wales studio to imagine a new threshold for the Red Centre building in the Kensington campus as they "proposed a surface intervention based on the conceptual wall of their choice. This was

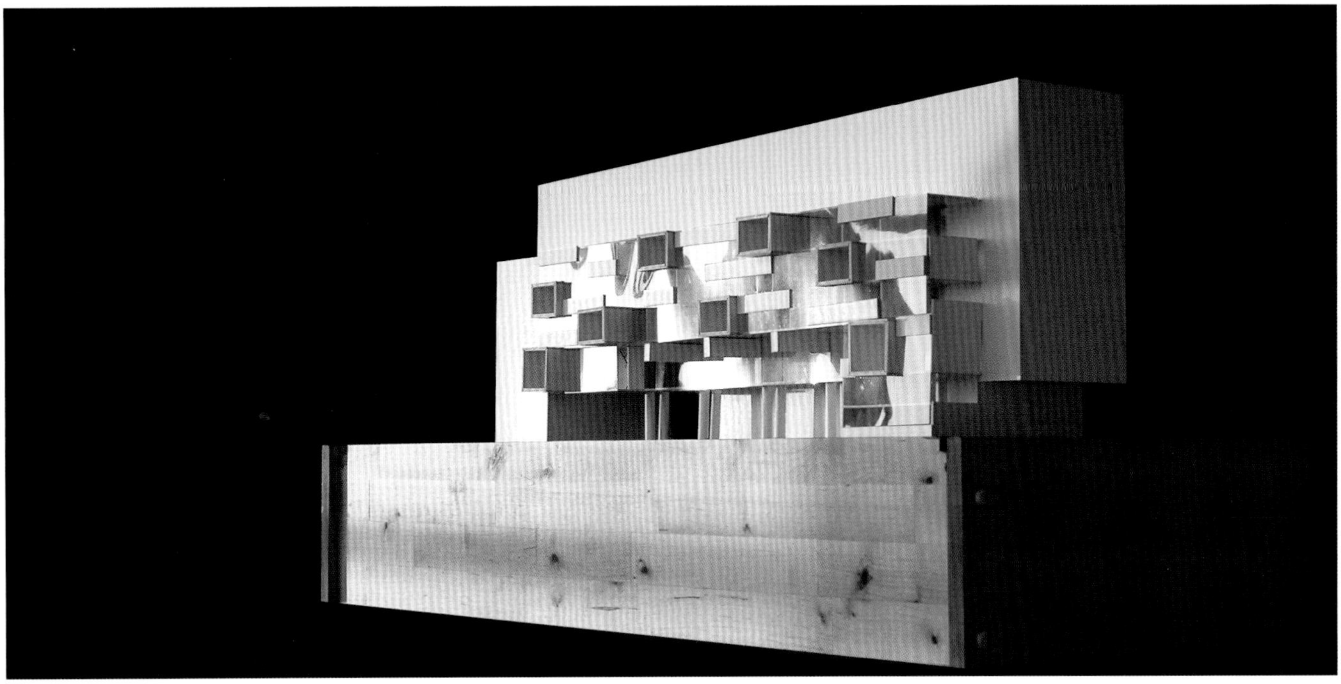

Figure 7
(Re)thinking and (Re) making the Threshold Studio—model showing proposed refurbishment of the threshold, University of New South Wales, 2011

imposed and impressed upon the existing structure. A given organizational order was infected and contaminated with another, with the aim of introducing a shift in the building's occupation, appearance, and experience, without a complete overhaul of the original building. The project was to be imagined variously as an extension, addition, insertion, and wrapping."[52] The research question posed by this studio was: What happens when we design with models outside in, infecting an existing organizational order with a new one? What spatial and tectonic potentials and possibilities might that suggest, which a convention plan and orthographic based design process might not? (Figure 7)

5. Postscript: Architectural Curriculum in India

While my three propositions are manifestations of literary pedagogies in architecture, this postscript identifies areas of missed opportunities in architectural curriculum in India. The first is the area of field, ethnographic-based studies in architecture, which is an opportunity for students to empathize with people and their experiences and narrate their findings as stories which might give design proposals the soul that they often lack. Yet, a lot of student projects demonstrate a dispassionate, data-oriented mindset that takes the emotion and the particularities out because they cannot be generalized, and possibly because so much of architectural education is dominated by the visual and graphic documentation—which means that whatever does not have a visual form does not get represented.

Second, is the false binary between theory and practice in architecture curricula, as if education (like life) can ever be compartmentalized into units and modules. Theory subjects, usually assessed through an examination format, often have lesser credits and contact hours. It is no wonder then that they are treated with less importance and they tend to have lesser traction in students' overall educational experience and professional career after graduation.

Third, as discussed in my *Seminar Magazine* essay, there is a lot of ground to be covered in terms of decolonizing architectural pedagogies (feminist principles, climate change, liberatory, critical and radical thinking, challenging knowledge canons, subverting cartographic hegemonies, and so on), but without making space for this to happen through the process of repeatedly reading, writing, and discussing, this is never going to become possible.[53] The job of architects is to first think. This essay is a "call to action" for a literary emergency in architectural education.

Notes

1. David Spurr, *Architecture and Modern Literature* (United States: University of Michigan Press, 2012), 3.
2. Spurr, Architecture and Modern Literature, 49.
3. ibid, 87.
4. ibid, 88.
5. Roger Thiel, "Architecture," in *Franz Kafka in Context*, ed. Carolin Duttlinger (United Kingdom: Cambridge University Press, 2017), 139.
6. Thiel, "Architecture," 143.
7. ibid.
8. Peta Mitchell, "Constructing the Architext: Georges Perec's Life a User's Manual," *Mosaic: A Journal for the Interdisciplinary Study of Literature* 37, no. 1 (2004): 2.
9. Mitchell, "Constructing the Architext," 3.
10. ibid, 2.
11. ibid, 3.
12. ibid, 4.
13. Claire Jamieson and Rebecca Roberts-Hughes, "Two Modes of a Literary Architecture: Bernard Tschumi and Nigel Coates," *Arq: Architectural Research Quarterly* 19, no. 2 (2015): 112.

14. Jamieson and Roberts-Hughes, "Two modes of a Literary Architecture," 120.
15. ibid.
16. ibid.
17. ibid.
18. Sophia Psarra, *Architecture and Narrative: The Formation of Space and Cultural Meaning* (Abingdon; New York: Routledge, 2009), 1.
19. ibid, 2.
20. ibid, 4.
21. ibid.
22. This section is sourced from Anuradha Chatterjee, "Notes on Literary Futures in Architecture," in *Unbuilt 2.0: Architecture of Future Collectives*, eds. Maanasi Hattangadi and Rajesh Advani (Delhi, India: ArchiSHOTS, 2021), 135–139.
23. Jane Rendell, "SITE-WRITING," Lecture transcript, https://janerendell.co.uk/wp-content/uploads/2013/02/Rendell-Site-Writing-PDF.pdf, accessed February 8, 2023.
24. Anna Ryan, "Writing Architecture," in *Patterns of Thought*, eds. Ellen Rowley and Maxim Laroussi (Dublin, Ireland: Architecture Republic, 2012): 345. Also see, Jennifer Bloomer, *Architecture and the Text: The (s)Crypts of Joyce and Piranesi* (United States: Yale University Press, 1993), 6.
25. Ryan, "Writing Architecture," 345–346.
26. See Rem Koolhaas, "Why I Wrote Delirious New York and other Textual Strategies. Interviewed by Cynthia Davidson," *Any* (1993), 42–43 (http://www.jstor.org/stable/41845557. accessed 3 Sept. 2023). See also, Chatterjee, "Notes on Literary Futures in Architecture," 138–139.
27. See Matthew Beaumont, "'A Little Political World of My Own': The New Woman, the New Life, and 'New Amazonia,'" *Victorian Literature and Culture* 35, no. 1 (2007): 215–232. This paragraph is sourced from Anuradha Chatterjee and Elisa Bizzoto, "Feminist Urban Utopias in the Literature of the Long Fin de Siècle: Inter-Cultural and Interdisciplinary Perspectives" (call for papers, unpublished).
28. Jennifer Sue Boyers, "Sexual Politics and Subversion: Feminist Utopia as Praxis" (PhD dissertation, Western Michigan University, 1998), 3.
29. Thomas Lewton, "Feminist Visions of Science and Utopia in Rokeya Sakhawat Hossain's 'Sultana's Dream,'" Features, Lady Science, 2019, science, https://www.ladyscience.com/features/feminist-visions-science-fiction-utopia-rokeya-hossain.
30. Maitrayee Chaudhuri, "Ecology and Virtue in Rokeya Sakhawat Hussain, Sultana's Dream," in *Feminist Moments: Reading Feminist Texts*, eds. Katherine Smits and Susan Bruce (London, United Kingdom: Bloomsbury Academic, 2016), 109.
31. Léone Drapeaud, "Founding the Feminist Utopia," *Site Magazine*, November 9, 2018, https://www.thesitemagazine.com/read/founding-the-feminist-utopia, accessed 10 March 2023.
32 This paragraph was first published in Anuradha Chatterjee, "Putting Her in Her Place (Not!)," *Veranda: Journal of Sushant School of Art and Architecture*, vol. 2 (2020), 88.
33. Linda N Groat and David Wang, *Architectural Research Methods*, Second edition (New Jersey, United States: John Wiley & Sons, Inc., 2013), 8.
34. Murray Fraser, *Design Research in Architecture: An Overview* (London, United Kingdom: Routledge, 2021), 2; David Salomon, "Experimental Cultures: On the 'End' of the Design Thesis and the Rise of the Research Studio," *Journal of Architectural Education*, 65, no. 1 (2011): 33–44.
35. Amritha Ballal, "What Could Have Been, What Can Be: How the Realm of the Architectural Unbuilt can Shape the Way We Build," in *India: Unbuilt Architecture* Vol 1, eds. Rajesh Advani and Ruturaj Parikh (New Delhi, India: Archishots, 2019), 76–80.
36. Michael U Hensel and Fredrik Nilsson, *The Changing Shape of Practice: Integrating Research and Design in Architecture* (London; New York: Routledge, 2016), 2.
37. Flora Samuel and Anne Dye, *Demystifying Architectural Research* (Newcastle upon Tyne: RIBA Publishing, 2015), ix.
38. Hensel and Nilsson, *The Changing Shape of Practice*, 23.
39. Katharine A Martindale, *Research for Architectural Practice* (Abingdon, Oxon; New York Routledge, 2022), vii.
40. Eireen Schreurs, Eva Storgaard, Marjan Michels, eds., *The Hybrid Practitioner: Building Teaching Researching Architecture* (Belgium: Leuven University Press, 2022).
41. Andrew Clancy, "Critical Practice: Can Architecture be Critical?" *The Architectural Review*, 2020, https://www.architectural-review.com/essays/in-practice/critical-practice-can-architecture-be-critical.
42. Beatriz Colomina, et al., eds., *Radical Pedagogies* (Massachusetts, United States: MIT Press, 2022), 11.
43. See James Graham, "The Critic as Producer: An Essay on Essays on Architecture," *The Avery Review 1* (2014): 1–7, https://averyreview.com/issues/1/the-critic-as-producer.
44. In reference to research on surface architecture, see Anuradha Chatterjee, *John Ruskin and the Fabric of Architecture* (London, United Kingdom: Routledge, 2017) and Anuradha Chatterjee, ed., *Surface and Deep Histories: Critiques, and Practices in Art, Architecture, and Design* (Newcastle upon Tyne: Cambridge Scholars Publishing, 2014).
45. Hélène Frichot and Naomi Stead, *Writing Architectures: Ficto-Critical Approaches* (London, United Kingdom: Bloomsbury Visual Arts, 2020), 11.
46. Klaske Havik and Angeliki Sioli, "Stories for Architectural Imagination," *Journal of Architectural Education* 75, no. 2 (2021): 168.
47. Beyhan Bolak Hisarligil, "Franz Kafka in the Design Studio: A Hermeneutic-Phenomenological Approach to Architectural Design Education," *International Journal of Art and Design Education* 31, no. 3 (2012): 257.
48. The studio culminated in an award-winning chapter (AMPS Routledge Pedagogy Award 2022) published as Anuradha Chatterjee, "In between Fiction and Space: Feminist Studio Pedagogy (of Letting Go)," in *Architectural Education: Catalysts and Tensions*, ed., Kasia Nawratek (London, United Kingdom: Routledge, 2022).
49. Koolhaas, "Why I Wrote Delirious New York," 2. See Salomon, "Experimental Cultures."
50. This studio led to a peer reviewed publication. See Anuradha Chatterjee, "Ungraspable Criticality: Surface in Architecture," *The Routledge Companion to Criticality in Art, Architecture and Design*, eds., Chris Brisbin and Myra Thiessen (London; New York: Routledge, 2020): 257–277.
51. See Anuradha Chatterjee, ed., *Surface and Deep Histories: Critiques, and Practices in Art, Architecture, and Design.*
52. Chatterjee, "Ungraspable Criticality: Surface in Architecture," 268.
53. See Anuradha Chatterjee, "Decolonizing Architectural Pedagogies," *Seminar: The Monthly Symposium*, ed., Vidhu Gandhi, no. 750 (February 2022): 53–56.

Figure Credits

Figure 1: Naman Pandey, *Glancing through History*, published September 13, 2020 (https://unsplash.com/photos/XwiKgYLyZHc, free to use under the Unsplash License).
Figure 2: Shanghai field trip drawing 1, Haoxuan Li, 2014; submitted to Xi'an Jiaotong Liverpool University (photo courtesy of Haoxuan Li).
Figure 3: Shanghai field trip drawing 2, Haoxuan Li, 2014; submitted to Xi'an Jiaotong Liverpool University (photo courtesy of Haoxuan Li).
Figure 4: Tabletop installation of graphic tiles from M. Mukundan's novel, *On the Banks of the Mayyazhi* by students of Avani Institute of Design, 2019 (author's photo).
Figure 5: Studio Instagram (sensing space) showing tectonic explorations by students of Avani Institute of Design, 2019 (author's image).
Figure 6: (Re)thinking and (Re)making the Threshold Studio—montage showing application of conceptual wall to the existing building, University of New South Wales, 2011; photo by student team: Lu Gan, Christopher Bloor, Jiaze Lu, and Thi Y Tho Nguyen (photo courtesy of Christopher Bloor).
Figure 7: (Re)thinking and (Re)making the Threshold Studio—model showing proposed refurbishment of the threshold, University of New South Wales, 2011; photo by student team: Lu Gan, Christopher Bloor, Jiaze Lu, and Thi Y Tho Nguyen (photo courtesy of Christopher Bloor).

The Architecture of Writing and Criticism

Michael J. CROSBIE, University of Hartford in West Hartford

Michael J. Crosbie, Ph.D., FAIA, NOMA, DPACSA studied architecture at the Catholic University of America and he is currently Professor of Architecture at the University of Hartford. He is the former editor of *Faith & Form: The Interfaith Journal on Religion, Art, and Architecture*. Dr Crosbie is the sole author, editor, or contributor to more than 75 books on architecture. The author of hundreds of articles on architecture, design, and practice, he lectures throughout the US and abroad. He is the recipient of the Edward S. Frey Memorial Award, "in Recognition of the Contributions Made to Religion, Art, and Architecture," bestowed by the American Institute of Architects. He is also a member of the AIA College of Fellows and received the Distinguished Professor Award from the Association of Collegiate Schools of Architecture. Dr Crosbie served as the Walton Visiting Critic at the Catholic University of America in 2015.

Abstract

The literature of architecture criticism is attached with a long history. The 1960s and '70s saw a boon in the criticism of architecture in newspapers for public consumption. Professional magazines provided coverage of architecture as well, but with less critical analysis. The number of architecture critics also expanded through the end of the twentieth century, but contracted as dailies cut staff, merged, or folded. However, over time, the number of critics online expanded, and sources of architectural commentary grew.

Professional architecture critics operate far less as gatekeepers and arbiters of taste. More criticism and commentary focus on the quality of urban life and sustainability. Lay people, too, feel empowered to assess architecture that affects them directly and more "citizen critics" engage with the built environment. Writer Wayne Attoe, in his book, *Architecture and Critical Imagination*, offers a framework for architecture criticism that removes it from the professional writer and allows it to flourish among people. His framework might, in fact, encourage more citizen critics to flourish. This paper, while offering a holistic view on architecture writing and criticism, also takes a close look at its development in the United States.

Author Information
Michael J. CROSBIE: crosbie@hartford.edu

Keywords

Architecture writing, architecture criticism, lay critic, professional critic.

1. Introduction

Architectural literature has a long history—nearly 2,000 years—one might argue, starting with Vitruvius's *The Ten Books of Architecture*, where he stated that architecture must possess "soundness, utility, and attractiveness" (according to Ingrid Rowland's translation of the Latin edition).

In the United States, architecture writing and criticism date back to the mid-1800s. In the 1960s and '70s, there was a boon in architecture criticism for public consumption as many newspapers instituted regular coverage of architecture, planning, and design. Professional magazines provided coverage of architecture, too, but with a less critical analysis than that found in daily newspapers. The number of architecture critics expanded through the end of the last century, with nearly forty writing on a regular basis at that time. In the past twelve years or so, however, the number of critics has contracted, as daily newspapers have cut staff, merged with other publications, or folded entirely. The irony is that, in the interim, the output of writers available online on the topic of architecture has expanded, as it is now more available through list-serves, Tweets, and blogs. While the number of professional architecture critics shrinks, the availability of architectural commentary grows, with many amateurs entering the field. Today, the professional architecture critic operates far less as a gatekeeper and an arbiter of taste. There is a growing trend of criticism and commentary focusing less on architectural style and more on the quality of urban life and sustainability the architecture affords. More lay people feel empowered to assess architecture that affects them directly and there are now more "citizen critics" or "lay critics" engaged with the built environment.

2. Early Architectural Writing

Architecture criticism in America traces its formal beginnings to the work of Montgomery Schuyler, who is considered one of the earliest and finest writers of architecture criticism in the US. In 1865, he joined *The World*, a biweekly newspaper, and 18 years later, moved to the *New York Times* and enjoyed a prolific career contributing to other publications as well, such as *Harper's Magazine*.

Schuyler also wrote for *Architectural Record* (Figure 1, page 39) (which is still published), where his biting criticism was unleashed in a series of columns called "Architectural Aberrations," in which he took architects to task for pathetic design work. However, the identity of the designers was usually not mentioned in the article out of professional courtesy. In 1930, the architectural historian and writer Talbot Hamlin lamented that, in comparison to the "bold days" of Schuyler, contemporary architecture criticism had become vapid, with writers who "can only smile at each other like women at a tea party whose external good manners hide a multitude of jealousies." Hamlin blamed the litigious nature of thin-skinned architects and developers for critics pulling their punches.[1]

In longing for the good "bad old" days of the aggressive architecture criticism of Schuyler, Hamlin conveyed a certain view of the architecture critic as one who anoints; one who passes judgment and admits the designer to a heavenly pantheon of architects who "have arrived" in a celestial realm of the celebrated. The architect might be a great talent, but it is the architecture critic who pronounces this greatness and sanctions it.

Such a view of the architecture critic as the gatekeeper to this celestial realm congealed in post-war America and was given a personality by the writer Ayn Rand, who is perhaps best remembered as the author of *The Fountainhead*, a novel about the triumph of individual genius over the rabble of mediocre talents. Rand chose an architect as the hero of her book. She described her protagonist Howard Roark as the personification of the ideal man—one of vision and of purpose, who cannot be swayed by the public opinion, indeed; anyone's opinion, including that of an architecture critic.

The book appeared in 1943 and the movie starring Gary Copper was released in 1949. The movie was not a commercial success, but the book and the movie inspired many young people to become architects. For example, architect and educator Fred Stitt, the founder of the San Francisco Institute of Architecture, dedicated a book to "his first architectural mentor, Howard Roark."
The architectural photographer Julius Schulman describes *The Fountainhead* as "first, front, and center in the life of every architect who was a modern architect." Why? I suspect it is because Roark was completely uncompromised. He did his work his way and would not change it for anyone. Essentially, he is every architect's dream. No one loved architecture more that Howard Roark. In considering Roark, Peter Keating—the fawning, weak, compromised architect in Rand's book—describes him this way: "He's a maniac on the subject of architecture. It seems to mean so damn much to him that he's lost all human perspective." If you asked Roark what he would do if he couldn't be an architect, Keating reflects: "He would walk over corpses. Any and all of them. All of us. But he'd be an architect."

If Howard Roark is the reason why some architects became architects, I would argue that Ellsworth Monkton Toohey is perhaps the reason why many architecture critics became critics. So who is Ellsworth Toohey? In *The Fountainhead*, he is the influential architecture critic for the *New York Banner*, the most powerful newspaper in the city, and he is Roark's chief nemesis. When *The Fountainhead* appeared in 1943, no American newspaper had a full-time architecture critic (the *New York Times* didn't have one until 20 years later). The Toohey character was a path-breaking invention.

Toohey makes and breaks architectural careers, promotes young architects and their work, and ensures that the best commissions for the most prestigious projects go to his protégées. Peter Keating is one of the architects he promotes, and Keating is swept up in Toohey's power brokering. In a meeting with the architecture critic, Keating reveals: "I always hoped that I would please you, that you'd approve of me, of my work. I even thought so often, when drawing, 'is this the kind of a building Ellsworth Toohey would say is good?'" This is heady stuff for any would-be architecture writer. Which critic wouldn't want to be the gatekeeper, the anointer?

In Rand's book, Toohey has sworn to ruin Roark because of the architect's unrelenting dedication to modern architecture and the triumph of his ego. And he has the power to do it too. But Roark really doesn't care. He doesn't need Toohey. He takes his commissions as he finds them, or his clients find him, on his own merits, without compromise. Toohey arranges for a commission to go to Roark, only to sabotage the work through a smear campaign in the *New York Banner*. Public opinion turns against the building and against Roark, whose practice is in shambles, thanks to Toohey.

One night, as Roark surveys the construction of a building designed by a competitor—selected by Toohey—the writer approaches Roark, to survey the damage he had done to the architect. "Mr Roark," says Toohey, "Why don't you tell me what

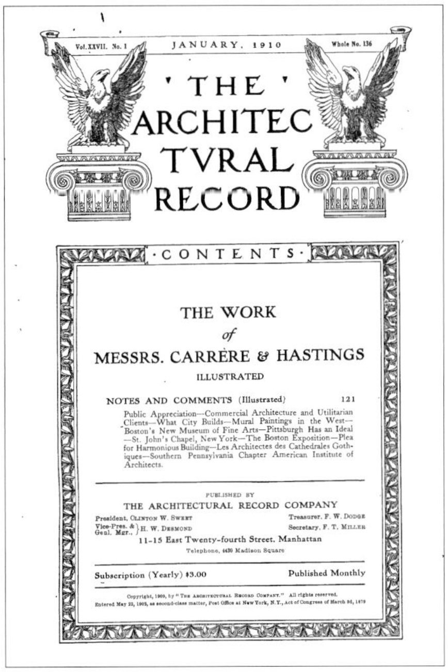

Vol. XXVII. No. 1 JANUARY, 1910 Whole No. 136

THE ARCHITECTVRAL RECORD

· CONTENTS ·

THE WORK *of* MESSRS. CARRÈRE & HASTINGS

ILLUSTRATED

NOTES AND COMMENTS (Illustrated) 121

Public Appreciation—Commercial Architecture and Utilitarian Clients—What City Builds—Mural Paintings in the West—Boston's New Museum of Fine Arts—Pittsburgh Has an Ideal—St. John's Chapel, New York—The Boston Exposition—Plea for Harmonious Building—Les Architectes des Cathedrales Gothiques—Southern Pennsylvania Chapter American Institute of Architects.

PUBLISHED BY

THE ARCHITECTURAL RECORD COMPANY

President, CLINTON W. SWEET — Treasurer, F. W. DODGE

Vice-Pres. & Genl. Mgr., H. W. DESMOND — Secretary, F. T. MILLER

11-15 East Twenty-fourth Street, Manhattan

Telephone, 4430 Madison Square

Subscription (Yearly) $3.00 — Published Monthly

Copyright, 1909, by "The Architectural Record Company." All rights reserved.

Entered May 22, 1902, as second-class matter, Post Office at New York, N.Y., Act of Congress of March 3d, 1879

Figure 1
Contents page of the January 1910 edition of *Architectural Record*, one of the leading architectural publications of the late nineteenth to early twentieth century

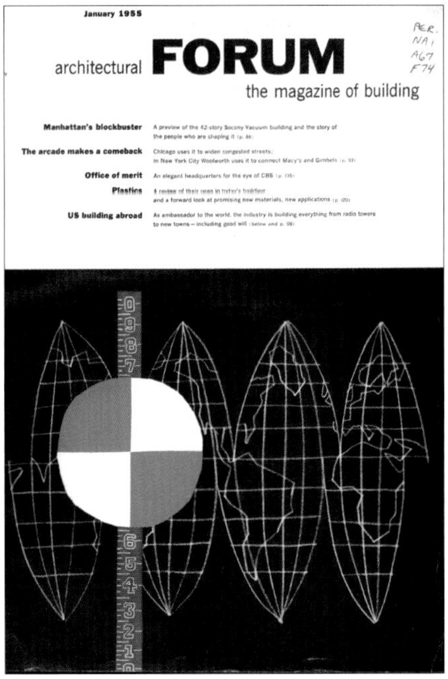

Figure 2
Cover of the January 1955 issue of *Architectural Forum*, one of several professional journals that rose to prominence in the mid-twentieth century

you think of me. In any words you wish. No one will hear us." Roark stares directly at the architecture critic, and says, "But I don't think of you." The architect triumphs over the critic.

Just about that time Hamlin wrote about weak-willed architecture critics in *American Architect*, a periodical on architecture; in 1931, Lewis Mumford started writing his "Skyline" column for *The New Yorker*, an American magazine; he continued writing the column for more than 30 years. Some have proposed that Rand modeled Ellsworth Toohey after Mumford. Mumford was not trained as an architect, but he was extremely well-read and reflective, influenced by the work of Scottish planner Patrick Geddes. Mumford wrote with passion about architecture, planning, and design; as an expression of social values and how it contributed to the quality of life. His focus was on civic space and civic life, but he also made connections between the ways society built and how it affected individual lives. After Mumford stopped writing his "Skyline" column in 1960, the column carried the criticism of other writers such as Brendan Gill and Paul Goldberger. But the absence of Mumford's voice in the '60s created a vacuum of commentary about the quality of the urban environment at a time when the public's awareness was heightened to what was happening to American cities through urban renewal.

3. Dedicated Architecture Criticism

The earliest, frequently published criticism in a daily newspaper about the built environment focused more on what was happening to the shape of cities in post-war America. Regular, serious attention to environmental design issues in American newspapers was initiated by Grady Clay at the *Louisville Courier-Journal* in Kentucky. He became the editor for news on real estate in 1950, reporting on national trends in real estate, urban renewal, suburbia, and the highway system. Clay later created the post of urban affairs editor, which he held until 1960. Another early architecture critic was George McCue, who wrote as the urban design and art critic for the *St. Louis Post-Dispatch* from about 1956.

The *Washington Post* and the *New York Times* added their own architecture critics in the early 1960s. Wolf von Eckardt was hired by the *Post* in 1963, the same year Ada Louise Huxtable began regular columns for the *New York Times* as a full time architecture critic. In 1996 Goldberger observed that, "Before Ada Louise Huxtable, architecture was not a part of the public dialogue," but this is not entirely accurate. Maybe it wasn't part of the public dialogue in New York City. Huxtable became the most visible architecture critic in the country, but others were writing about architecture and urban design in American newspapers long before she took up her pen at the *New York Times*.

The fledgling preservation movement in the 1960s raised the consciousness of many about what our cities might lose in the wake of post-war construction. Huxtable wrote as an architecture critic for the *Times* until 1982, and later took the position of architecture critic at the *Wall Street Journal*. Other critical voices were raised in other cities: Allen Temko at the *San Francisco Chronicle* wrote in a visceral fashion about architecture from 1961 to 1993 and Paul Gapp wrote about architecture for the *Chicago Tribune* from 1974 to 1992. All gained large followings of readers. The number of critics grew in the 1980s, when postmodernism caught the public's imagination. By 2001, a study of the work of architecture critics by the Columbia University School of Journalism included critics from thirty-seven newspapers around the country.

Today, we live in a much different world of architecture criticism than we did just a decade or more ago. While there are far fewer newspapers with dedicated architecture critics (and far fewer newspapers, period), paradoxically the access to reportage, criticism, and opinion about architecture and the built environment seems more abundant and widespread.

For example, the amount of writing about architecture and design available online seems to have only grown over the past decade. But the US critical climate still lags behind that seen in such places as the UK. In Great Britain, for example, between *The Guardian* and *The Observer*, there are about five critics writing about architecture on a regular basis.

Besides newspapers there are magazines and strictly online publications such as *ArchDaily* (one of the most visited architectural websites in the world). Most of today's dedicated architecture critics blog and tweet and post on other forms of social media as a way to promote their longer, polished reviews of architecture. For instance, Blair Kamin, the former architecture critic for the *Chicago Tribune*, has a little over 17,000 followers on Twitter; former *New Yorker* architecture critic, Paul Goldberger, has nearly 27,000 Twitter followers; the former *Los Angeles Times* critic Christopher Hawthorne has about 19,000 followers; Michael Kimmelman of the *New York Times* beats them all, he has 31,400.

The internet has given us an assortment of bloggers about architecture, architecture groupie websites, and LinkedIn groups dedicated to discussing architecture and its practice. Tripadvisor.com regularly runs "reviews" of architecturally significant sites around the world written by visitors to these landmarks. Sometimes, it seems as though everyone has become an architecture critic, or at least everyone has the potential to make their voice heard about what they think about architecture.

3.1 What's the Point?

What exactly is the point of architecture criticism? What does it mean to be critical? What function does architecture criticism perform? Does architecture criticism really make a difference? The answers to such questions depend on the outlet of criticism and the audience.

Criticism is derived from the Greek word *krinein*, meaning to separate, to sift, to make distinctions, to discern, to examine, or to judge. According to Wayne Attoe, who has written extensively on architecture criticism, this does not necessarily mean to disapprove of, or to find fault with. It can be favorable or non-favorable, it can praise or condemn. Our contemporary understanding of the word "criticism" tends to cast it in an unfavorable light. Architecture criticism, at its best, is discerning, which is not a bad thing at all. Attoe makes the distinction between criticism as a thing, which is a product which—particularly in American culture—usually means something negative, and criticism as a behavior.

As a behavior, criticism is a mode of seeing, of examining the particular way in which we assess the built world around us. The actual decision or judgment—good or bad—is less a function of criticism than a result of the critique. Criticism is a behavior, not a judgment, Attoe contends. If you think of it this way, it is easy to understand why people who write about architecture are always "on," so to speak. Being critical is their typical *modus operandi*. Asking a critic to stop being critical is like my asking you to stop seeing the colors green or blue. It's the way the writer beholds the world.

In the best of all possible circumstances, writes Attoe, criticism should be a tool for generating better work. He believes that the key to achieving this understanding of criticism, which he sees as a tool and not a threat, is to see criticism as a behavior and not a judgment. When it comes to being critical of criticism, Attoe observes: "Criticism will always be more useful when it informs the future than when it scores the past."[2] So how is criticism useful in informing the future and to make better work possible—essentially, to make a difference in the quality of the built environment?

Critics themselves are not much help in regard to criticism's usefulness. Goldberger, the man who is today considered the "dean" of American architecture critics, says: "I don't think criticism matters very much." He qualifies this view by adding that it doesn't matter in the way that many critics and architects want it to matter: it doesn't change the world. He believes that it doesn't even change the nature of architecture all that much. He draws parallels to theater criticism, noting that if a drama critic pans a Broadway show it could very well close. "Nobody tears down a building if the architecture critic doesn't like it."[3]

Even the late architect and critic Michael Sorkin, who wrote about architecture for the *Village Voice* in the 1980s said: "I flatly refuse to acknowledge having had any impact at all in the real world."[4]

A few years ago, Columbia University's School of Journalism (United States) undertook a survey of architecture critics, asking if their writing matters. While more than three-quarters of the critics surveyed felt that their writing had some impact on architecture in the region, more than half said that architects and developers don't consider their options when designing new projects.[5] Many architecture writers and critics see their role as an "informant" rather than as a "judge," educating the public on what the architect or the client were trying to achieve on a project and perhaps judging on these merits. Critics in the Columbia study also saw their writing as an "early warning system" to alert a community to new projects in process, helping the public to be aware and to take action.[6]

Other critics express a missionary spirit about what they do, and whether it matters. Martin Filler, who writes about architecture for *The New York Review* says that, "The highest goal of the critic ought to be to make people think about their environment and to participate more actively—by joining a community planning board, picketing to save a landmark, trying to change zoning laws, or establishing a historic district—that's what I think a critic should do."[7]

Kamin, the former *Chicago Tribune* critic, echoes Filler in this regard when he reflects on the contributions of Temko, who wrote about architecture for the *San Francisco Chronicle* for more than 30 years. Kamin describes how Temko would get out in front of projects in the planning stage before the damage could be done. According to Kamin: "This sort of preemptive strike—not waiting for mistakes to happen, but going after them before it was too late—had an enormous impact. It resulted not simply in better bridges, but in better architecture, better historic preservation, [and] better waterfront and coastal protection. As Temko showed, confronting bad plans head on—and doing it on your home turf, week after week, year after year—is the ultimate test of a critic's mettle."[8]

In addition to acting as a translator who communicates between the architecture profession and the public, and as a gatekeeper of architecture for the public who selects and filters architectural ideas for public consumption (two roles that Goldberger identifies among the architecture critic's duties), the best architecture critic must also be a bit of a street tough. The British architecture historian and critic Joseph Rykwert writes that he "always believed that the critic must be a fighter. To do so they must have a base from which to operate, not only the obvious one of a newspaper ... or blog which will make their views public, but more intimately, a clearly articulated notion of what they think society must expect of its builders."[9] As Rykwert observes, a good critic situates himself or herself into the community, sort of on a neighborhood watch for bad architecture. This lack of a position in a community or being distracted by the high-flying "starchitecture" of jet-setting practitioners was among the complaints people harbored against former *New York Times* architecture critic Nicolai Ouroussoff, who seemed not all that interested in writing about architecture in New York.

4. The Editor's Role

Critiques of the state of architecture criticism focus almost exclusively on the work of the professional critics, and rarely consider the powers behind the publications that shape the critique. Publication editors, of course, play a significant role in setting the topics that are covered and how they are covered. The extent of that power can vary widely, depending on the publication and the intended audience of the criticism.

Architecture critics at news outlets and general interest publications complain that editors don't understand architecture enough. The irony is that architecture, as the most public art, is probably the least understood by the general public, and professional editors are not too far behind. They often lack knowledge or even interest. Editors always want to know what "the hook" is: Is the building a part of a trend? Is there some other general interest angle to justify running a story?[10]

The result is that editors at news outlets and general interest publications sometimes gravitate toward covering architectural celebrities with profiles of star architects, talking about personalities instead of design.

Editors of magazines targeted to an audience of architectural professionals, particularly print journals such as *Architect* and *Architectural Record*, still act as gatekeepers to access in two directions: access of architectural designers to see their works published, and access of readers to the work of architects whose work was deemed worthy of attention by the editors. In some ways, the editor often assumes a curatorial posture; young architects and their work can be "discovered" and then promoted by editors. But the best editors, particularly the ones for professional journals, consistently look for balance, for un-heard voices or under-appreciated designers. They try to present diverse points of view and do not attempt to promote a monolithic view of architecture (if such a thing is even possible anymore). As editors, they challenge themselves, and they are willing to be surprised. They make well-reasoned decisions on what to publish and what not to publish, and they routinely go back and re-check those decisions to ensure if the logic is still sound or has somehow become flimsy with the shifting landscape of new design work. They also seek out new critical voices and new emerging critics. The editor can function here as a curator as well, identifying new writing talent and giving it space.

If editors of general interest publications might care too little about architecture, you could argue that editors of professional architectural publications care too much. Competition within the field, especially in the days of exclusively print journals such as *Architecture*, *Architecture Forum* (Figure 2, page 39), *Architecture Plus*, *Architectural Record*, and *Progressive Architecture*, could be fierce, with publishers and editors vying for market share. This led to unethical journalistic practices, such as promising architects glossy covers, greater page counts for articles, the choice of writer, and even allowing the architects to review the text before publication, in exchange for exclusive coverage. Genuine criticism in the professional press was, and continues to be, virtually impossible under these conditions and the professional architecture press suffered (and continues to suffer) for it.

The multitude of sources of information on new architecture today makes the exclusivity of professional journals completely useless. But old habits die hard. Professional journals seem edgier and more willing to take risks today. I believe that the reason for this is partly to differentiate themselves in a field populated by online publications, bloggers, Tweeters, Tumblrs, Instagrammers, Tik-Tokers, Pinterest junkies, and the like. *Progressive Architecture*, an American magazine on architecture and design was an early adopter of this approach, radically changing in the early 1990s the way architecture was presented and critiqued. Under the leadership of Tom Fisher, who became executive editor in 1992 sharing editorial direction with John Morris Dixon, the magazine took what I believe to be a bold direction in not only publishing tougher critiques, but also in addressing issues in the profession that had been off limits: gender, exploitation of interns, the ineffectiveness of the national American Institute of Architects (Figure 3, page 42), licensing practices, architectural education, and design awards programs. The focus became more "investigative," producing articles that dug into the issues, targeting some of the profession's sacred cows.

5. What Happens Next?

We are at a point where the nature of architecture criticism is changing from one that has been practiced by professional critics writing for publications that are essentially "gatekeepers" and formers of public opinion about buildings, to one where architecture criticism is more diffused, egalitarian, accessible, democratic, chaotic, opinionated, potentially misinformed, and maybe consequential. What I am describing, of course, is a landscape of discussion about architecture that looks very much like other realms: politics, sports, art, and movies. Commentary in every one of these fields, and many more, is undergoing a great leveling. There is simply too much free information out there in the digital public realm for anyone to act as an arbiter of taste. The critic has lost the gatekeeper job.

Where we go from here is anyone's educated guess, but I believe that the way we communicate and share information today has the potential to make every one of us an architecture critic. This does not mean that the quality of that criticism will always be worth reading, but there are many free things on the net that fascinate. And there are more ways today to learn how to be a critic if you wanted to be one. We already see signs of this in the wealth of travel blogs and posts on TripAdvisor about the architecture of the places where people vacation. There certainly seems to be an interest.

There is a hint of what might be next in *Writing About Architecture* by Alexandra Lange, which opens with a chapter called "How to Be an Architecture Critic." In it, Lange writes about how critics operate and structure their critique,

Figure 3
Progressive Architecture, April 1994: in the early 1990s, the journal regularly took on critical topics in the profession, such as the conduct of the American Institute of Architects

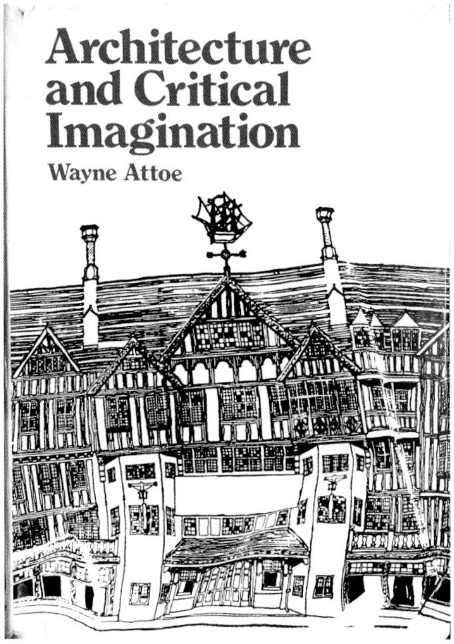

Figure 4
Writer Wayne Attoe presented a detailed and exhaustive taxonomy of the methods of criticism of the built environment in his book *Architecture and Critical Imagination*

and the methods they use. Lange's intent is not to create a future legion of Goldbergers, however. Where some architecture critics talk about educating the public about architecture, Lange's intent is to educate the public about criticism. What we need, she writes, "are more critics—citizen critics—equipped with the desire and the vocabulary to remake the city."[11]

6. Everyone's A Critic

While Lange offers her readers the work of noted commentators of the built environment—Huxtable, Mumford, Sorkin, Frederick Law Omsted, and Charles Moore—as touchstones of critique, a different approach is taken by Attoe, whose book, *Architecture and Critical Imagination* (Figure 4), predates Lange's by some 35 years and which has a broader mission: to transform each of us into a critic. Attoe's approach is far more inclusive. While Lange's conception of architecture criticism remains locked within the confines of a "review" produced by the architecture critic who writes it, Attoe asserts that architecture criticism is happening all the time, by everyone, if we chose to recognize it as such. He explains that in researching his book on architecture criticism, what surfaced was, "an almost sinful appreciation of all forms or response to the built environment and a willingness to say that if everything is criticism then the most one should expect of a critic is that the media he employs be suited to the ends pursued." Attoe notes that his "tolerance" for what he is willing to include as legitimate criticism is "the product of a particular point of view, namely that virtually everything people do in and about the built environment is a form of criticism." All of us, architects and non-architects, engage in criticism much of the time, through an "ongoing collection of diverse behaviors."[12]

Such a view of criticism can be liberating in the extreme. While it challenges our conception of architectural writing—having been produced by someone with specialized knowledge and experience, who is the only one anointed to pass judgment on works of architecture—it seems to be much more in line with the way people actually react to architecture—by embracing it or running from it. Such a recognition is evident in a variety of "critiques;" everything from post-occupancy building evaluations and the work of William Holly Whyte—who more than 50 years ago documented the life of urban spaces with a concealed 8-millimeter camera—to YouTube videos today of people interacting with the built world around them.

This form of interpretation of criticism demands an inclusive framework for criticism. Attoe provides an excellent one, categorizing the methods of criticism as "Normative"—using an outside system of standards for critique; "Interpretive"—seeking to make the reader see the building as the critic does; and "Descriptive"—focusing on factual information in as objective a way as possible.[13] This is a comprehensive framework for understanding the critical nature of many of our interactions with the built environment. For example, who knew that building inspectors could be architecture critics? But they are, interpreting the building codes as a form of Normative criticism. Photographers work as critics using the Interpretive method when they capture the special qualities of an old building, or a traditional neighborhood threatened by demolition. The Historic American Buildings Survey was instituted in 1933 as a form of Descriptive criticism, although it was never referred to in that way, documenting much of architecture's heritage.

Attoe even considers the work of the "Lay Critic," who are people who are not trained as professional critics or designers and who do not commission buildings and projects, but who interact with the built environment every day and practice their architecture criticism directly.

7. Lay Criticism

Lay Criticism is manifested in four areas: attitude toward the environment; adoptive behavior within the environment; unintentional modification of the environment; and intentional modification of the environment.[14] The first, "attitude toward the environment," is recorded in written or verbal responses in such forums as "Letters to the Editor," columns in publications, in personal blogs, Tweets, and comments about architectural articles that users respond to. You can also gauge attitude through surveys: for example, based on interviews with users, is the location and design of a public space inviting for people to be there? Adoptive behavior within the environment implies that the lay critic accepts it as is, without modification. Lay critics vote with their feet; they either flock to a public place or avoid it. They adopt it, make it their own, or they don't. Moore's Piazza D'Italia in New Orleans, United States, is a good example of a stage set for civic life that never lived up to its promise. Having visited it several times over the years, I have noted that it is always vacant. It was never adopted as a public space.

Unintentional modification of the environment happens when people unintentionally change the environments they use, without even realizing they are doing it. For example, the grass in a public park might be worn away connecting two points with a straight line—unintentional modification indicating a preference on the part of the pedestrian. Attoe calls this kind of unintentional modification "erosion." Another version of such criticism is "accretion." Finger marks on a building are evidence of people's interest in it, which is a good example. On the dedication wall of the East Building of the National Gallery of Art in Washington, D.C., United States, there is an accretion of oil from people's fingers touching the name of the building's architect, I.M. Pei. I would interpret this as evidence of the public's positive "critique" of Pei's design.

Intentional modification of the environment is a critique whereby the Lay Critic acts upon it, sometimes to improve it. In post-war Levittown in Long Island, New York, United States, cookie-cutter Cape Cod houses were modified over the years to the point where they are now all different, thanks to the changes residents made. Le Corbusier's multi-family housing project in Pessac, France, built in 1924, underwent a similar transformation, as homeowners intentionally modified units to make them more what they thought a "home" should be. A historian who studied these modifications writes: "Le Corbusier, who apparently considered this project a failure, stated that the tenant 'must change his outlook,' but unbeknownst to him, it was the tenant, who with great ease, changed the architecture."[15]

Intentional modification, and by extension lay architecture criticism, can also be a destructive commentary on the environment or the forces that have brought it about. We typically refer to this as vandalism, but vandalism can be idle, or it can be active; a way of engaging the environment with graphic commentary. It can be a form of lay architecture or social critique. Graffiti offers an outlet for a visceral critique of the environment around us. But if the built environment is too alienating and too inhuman, the ultimate end might demand destruction, as was the case of Pruitt-Igoe in St. Louis, Missouri, United States; the 1956 public housing development was finally dynamited in the 1970s.

8. Conclusion

For the past 40 years or so, I have taught a course, "Writing About Architecture," at a variety of architecture schools that is formulated on Attoe's taxonomy of architecture criticism. Students readily apprehend the usefulness of Attoe's framework, in that it allows them to critique the built environment using a variety of means beyond the written word. The point of my course is not to create new architecture critics in the formal, professional sense, but to help students be more critical of the built world, and to encourage them to articulate an architectural point of view or a philosophy of critique which they can then use as a lens to assess architecture—their own and that of others. This leads to a better educated architecture student and, ultimately, to a better architect; one who understands that they cannot be objective; that they see the world from a very personal vantage point; and that they can expect the same of others. No one can be an objective critic. I think E.B. White expressed it best when he wrote: "Whoever sets pen to paper writes of himself." And, I would add, even if she or he writes about architecture.

In a world where everyone is potentially an architecture critic, such tools are invaluable because they help us to organize our experiences and see what is there, as well as what might be. The poet Paul Éluard could have been describing the work of the architecture critic of the future, when he wrote, "There is another world, but it is in this one." The architecture critic hopes to make a difference, if not immediately in the built world around us, then, at least, in the built world inside each one of us.

Notes

1. Talbot Hamlin, "Criticism Might Help Architecture, Let's Try It." *American Architect*, May 1930, 41.
2. Wayne Attoe, *Architecture and Critical Imagination* (New York, United States: John Wiley & Sons, 1978), xii.
3. Paul Goldberger, "Architecture Criticism: Does it Matter?" accessed May 27, 2023, http://www.paulgoldberger.com/lectures/architecture-criticism-does-it-matter.
4. Suzanne Stephens, "Assessing the State of Architectural Criticism in Today's Press," *Architectural Record*, March 1998, 64–69.
5. András Szántó, Eric Fredericksen, and Ray Rinaldi, "The Architecture Critic: A Survey of Newspaper Architecture Critics in America," New York, United States: National Arts Journalism Program, Colombia University, 2001, 8.
6. ibid.
7. Gerald Sikes, "Critics on Criticism," *Metropolis*, November 1985, 28–29.
8. Blair Kamin, "Battling for Better Architecture: The Argument for Activist Criticism," *Architectural Record*, December 2006, 41–45.
9. Joseph Rykwert, "Does Architectural Criticism Matter?" *The Architects' Journal*, September 2012, 61–62.
10. Suzanne Stephens, "Assessing the State of Architectural Criticism in Today's Press," 64–69.
11. Alexandra Lange, *Writing About Architecture* (New York, United States: Princeton Architectural Press, 2012), 8.
12. Wayne Attoe, *Architecture and Critical Imagination*, xxii.
13. ibid, 9–10.
14. ibid, 154–161.
15. Phillippe Boudon, *Lived-In Architecture* (Massachusetts, United States: MIT Press, 1972).

Figure Credits

Figure 1: Contents page of the January 1910 edition of *Architectural Record*, one of the leading architectural publications of the late nineteenth to early twentieth century (author's photo).
Figure 2: Cover of the January 1955 issue of *Architectural Forum*, one of several professional journals that rose to prominence in the mid-twentieth century (author's photo).
Figure 3: *Progressive Architecture*, April 1994: in the early 1990s, the journal regularly took on critical topics in the profession, such as the conduct of the American Institute of Architects (author's photo).
Figure 4: Writer Wayne Attoe presented a detailed and exhaustive taxonomy of the methods of criticism of the built environment in his book *Architecture and Critical Imagination* (author's photo).

New State Courts

The building is highly open and visible to the public

Architect firm: Serie Architects, Multiply Architects and Engineers LLP
Principal consultant and architect: CPG Consultants Pte Ltd
Location: Havelock Square, Singapore
Area: 113,000 square meters
Completion date: 2019
Photography: Finbarr Fallon, Khoogj

Courtroom complexes are typically designed in a conservative manner, partly due to complex circulation requirements to keep the judges, persons-in-custody, and the public separate.

The new State Courts towers, however, in contrast, have been designed to be highly open and visible to the public. This is achieved with two architectural strategies.

First, the building is split into two slender towers connected by link bridges. The front tower accommodates courtrooms and the back tower the judges' chambers and staff offices. This architectural move not only brings light deep into the building, but also helps keep the circulation of the different entities separate.

The second strategy places the courtroom boxes on large, open "court trays." These trays are not only of different heights to fit courtrooms of different sizes, but also completely open—there is no glazed façade around the tower. Instead, each tray accommodates a lushly planted garden terrace that filters the tropical sun, while allowing views out over the city. As a result, the court tower appears light, open, and welcoming.

The courtrooms are clad in tall pigmented pre-cast panels measuring 5 to 12 meters in height, which have been inspired by the colors and textures of the tiled roofs in the historic shophouses in adjacent Chinatown, one of Singapore's heritage enclaves. The intention is to bring together two typical forms of architecture from the immediate area—namely the high-rise and the shophouses—into a single frame, so that the new building is at once familiar and yet excitingly new.

The office tower which houses working spaces is expressed as a thin and elegant slab tower. The façade features an expanding and contracting grid. Vertically, the grid contracts where the service core is located, and expands where light and views are required in the middle. The modulation of the horizontal grids draws the eye across the façade and toward the sky, shaping a clean and absolute form, and a sense of playful rhythm.

An entrance canopy opens up the site to the surrounding context and creates two entrances—the entrance from Havelock Square, and another from Upper Cross Street.

Commenting on the intricacies of court planning, Colin Wu, lead architect and senior vice president of CPG Consultants shares: "CPG has historically designed and constructed many of Singapore's present court buildings, such as the Supreme Court and Family Justice Courts. Our familiarity with court complex design and planning in Singapore helped us in designing the programmatic spaces, operations, and security requirements for this first, high-rise court complex. Our aim in this project was to ensure there is clear segregation in the programing of the three primary user groups: the judges, persons-in-custody, and the public."

The site for the new State Courts towers is also smaller, meaning that vertical court towers—as compared to a more common horizontal layout—had to be planned. This posed a challenge and careful planning and stacking of the fifty-three courtrooms and fifty-four hearing chambers was necessary to ensure that court operations would not be hindered in any way. One of the successful outcomes is the simplicity in the vertical stacking of those programs and circulation, which makes wayfinding easy for the public.

As a modern, IT-enabled courthouse, the complex also displays various smart building features like facial recognition, as well as the automation of various building management processes related to security, mechanical, and electrical systems. Other IT/web-enabled services include video-conferencing facilities and interactive self-service kiosks. A universal design approach ensures that, as a modern courthouse, the new State Courts towers is user-friendly to the judges, persons in custody, and public. For example, assistive listening systems are provided for court attendees in all the courtrooms, and digital wayfinding is also offered through the use of apps; there is also a child-minding facility.

The State Courts towers is also an environmentally sustainable building, with innovative green building features incorporated in its design, such as solar panels and condensate water recovery systems.

Two slender towers connected by 39-foot bridges

A juxtaposition of old and new creates interesting tension in the fabric of the exterior scenery

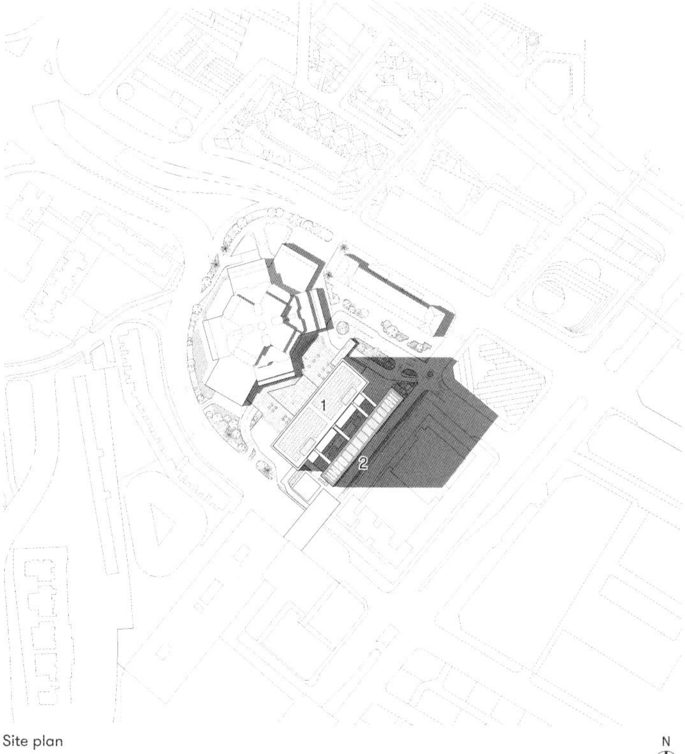

Site plan

1. The Courtroom Tower
2. The Office Tower housing judges' chambers and staff offices

The side of the entrance canopy that opens to Upper Cross Street

The façade features an expanding and contracting grid

The grid iterates a clean façade with a sense of playful rhythm

Rear view of the building

Entrance from Havelock Square

Lushly planted garden terraces surround the courtrooms

Courtrooms with pre-cast panels inspired by the terra cotta roofs of adjacent Chinatown

The courtrooms are clad in 6-meter-tall modular pigmented pre-cast panels

The modern and IT-enabled courthouse

Front view of courtrooms in different sizes with an open frame

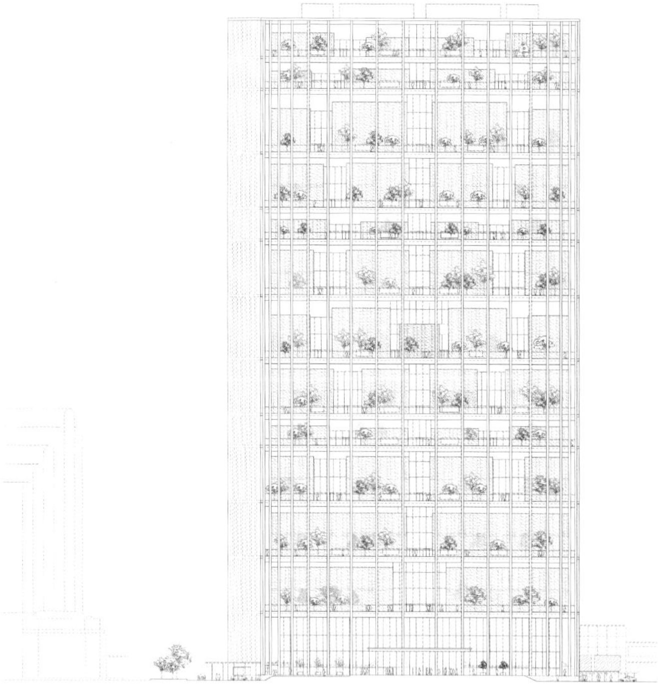
Front elevation

Façade of courtrooms inspired by the colors and textures of the tiled roofs in the historic shophouses in adjacent Chinatown

Huazhan Campus of Shanghai Gaoan Road No. 1 Primary School

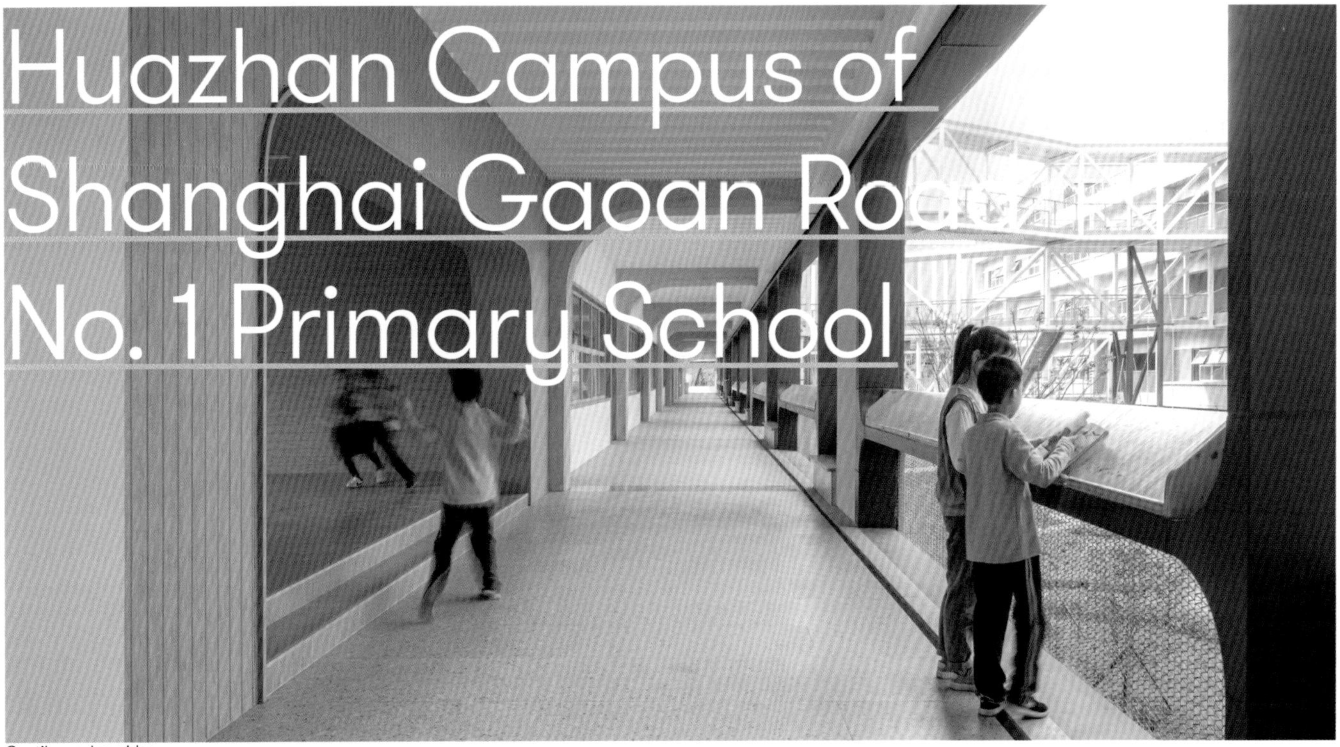

Cantilevered corridor

Architect firm: Scenic Architecture Office
Principal architect: Xiaofeng Zhu
Design team: Xiaofeng Zhu, Qitong Li, Yan Zhou, Xuan Zhang, Guohao Zhang, Xianmei Hu, Linfeng Xu, Ran He, Chunlin Huang, Keyu Tao
Location: Shanghai, China
Area: 30,406 square meters
Completion date: 2020
Photography: Shengliang Su

The Huazhan campus of Gaoan Road No. 1 Primary School is located in Shanghai, China. With a FAR (floor area ratio) of 1.4, the compact site accommodates one 200-meter track, a field, two classroom buildings, an office building, and a multifunction building which houses a multifunction hall, a covered sports field, a gymnasium, and other activity spaces.

The block is divided into four parts, with passages and staircases designed between them, to allow teachers and students to witness the scenery of different spaces inside and outside the campus.

To avoid the separation between the playground and the central courtyard caused by the multifunction building, the gymnasium has been lifted to the third floor, and the small theater has been lowered to the semi-underground level. Green slopes and grandstands have been placed on the periphery to reduce the impact of the large scale of the multifunction building and a covered sports field has been formed on the second floor. This semi-outdoor space is connected to the gymnasium atrium vertically, and to the playground and the central courtyard horizontally. Because the narrow and long central courtyard creates a sense of constriction, airy bridges have been added to strengthen the connection between the north and the south, and to change the proportions of the courtyard, bringing a spatial hierarchy to this wooded green space. Through these design strategies of transparency, a layered connection between the central courtyard and the surrounding space, and the external environment is established, and the spatial perception of the campus is expanded.

The gymnasium and the covered sports field in the multifunction building are large-span spaces. In order to meet the prefabrication rate and reduce the structural height, the main structure adopts a steel frame system supported by a shear wall to achieve an open floor. The inverted trapezoidal shear wall is retracted at the bottom to enlarge the view of the grandstand. The changing "aperture" openings on the shear walls dissolve the dullness of the structure and draw the eye. Since the school is former professional basketball player, Yao Ming's alma mater, dedicated attention is directed to the indoor gymnasium. Instead of using a truss or network frame structure, braces are used to assist the steel beam to complete a span of 23 meters. The triangular area formed by braces creates a semi-transparent space for ventilation and natural lighting, injecting a sort of spiritual brilliance into the gymnasium.

In order to control the overall cost, the concrete frame structure of the classroom building and office building adopt a combination of prefabricated and cast-in-place reinforced-concrete structures. Compared with ordinary prefabricated systems, this project features three new approaches: The use of a cantilever to support the outer corridor of the single-row classroom building in order to obtain a free interface between the corridor and the courtyard; the elimination of the secondary beams and ceilings by using prefabricated profiled reinforced-concrete composite slabs—the electrical pipelines and the sprinkler branch pipes can be laid along the grooves of the slabs, so that the classroom unit gains the largest clearance and integrality of the space; and the enlarging of the joints of the prefabricated reinforced-concrete beams and columns, which improves the reinforcement of the junctions. The structural element of the arch frames is constantly reproduced in school gates, lobbies, corridors, classrooms, cabins, libraries, and gymnasiums, becoming the motif of spatial shaping.

In the limited building area, the diversification of the circulation space promotes vitality in communication. The rope stair in the multifunction building, the semi-outdoor "cabins," and the corridor equipped with stools, schoolbag cabinets, and reading panels, together, provide unique public spaces.

The design explores the diversification and differentiation of teaching and communication spaces, and imputes to the extra thought on students' physical and mental well-being that went into the design of this campus.

Aerial view of campus

1. Sports field
2. Multifunction building
3. Classroom building
4. Courtyard
5. Office building

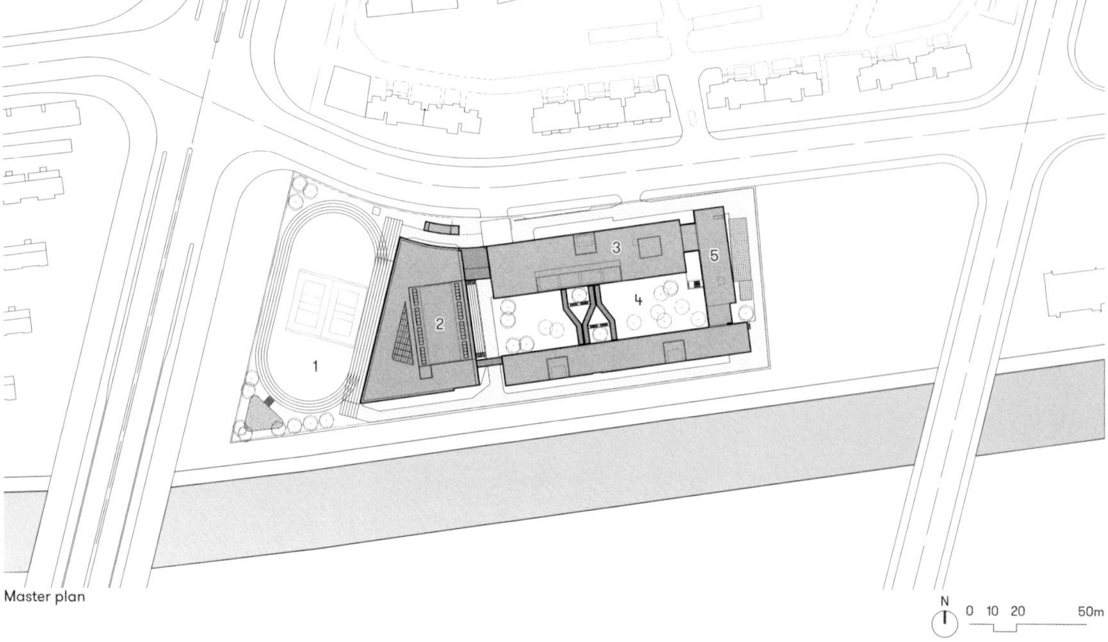

Master plan

Night view

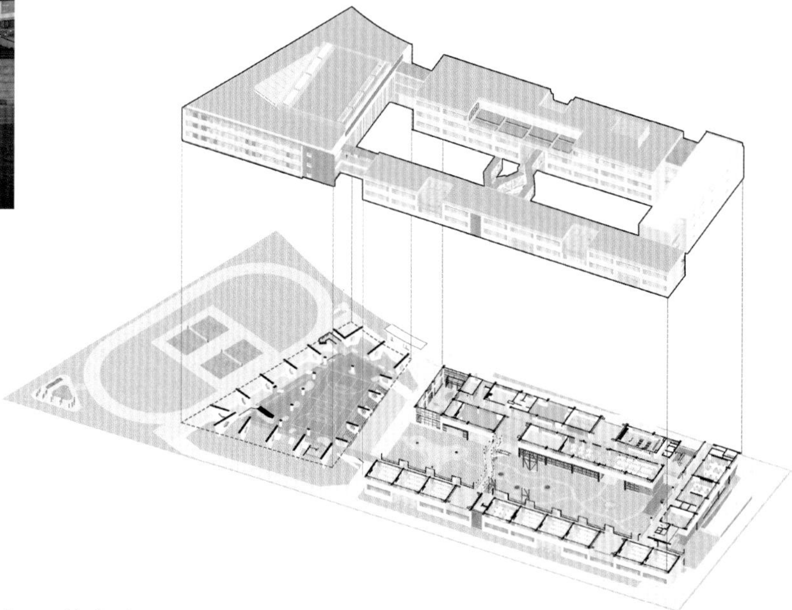
Axonometric drawing

The central courtyard

Corridor

Covered sports field

Free interface between the corridor and the courtyard

Rope stair in the multifunction building

View of the lobby

A class in session

Future laboratory

Gymnasium with exposed structural bones

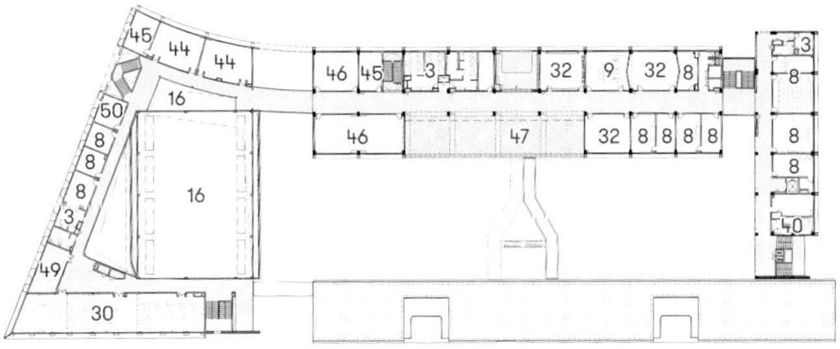

Fifth-floor plan

Various activity spaces along the corridor

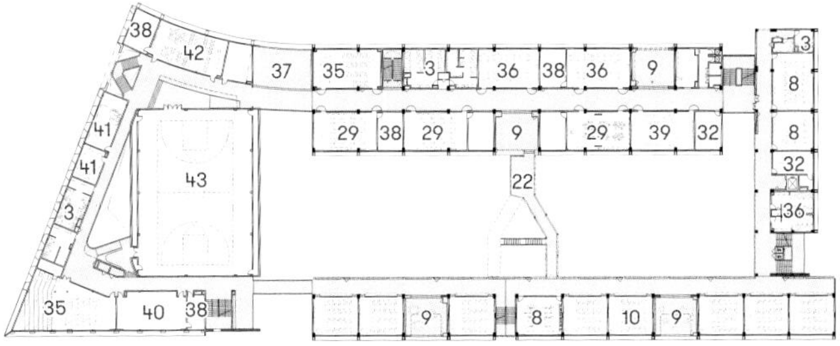

Fourth-floor plan

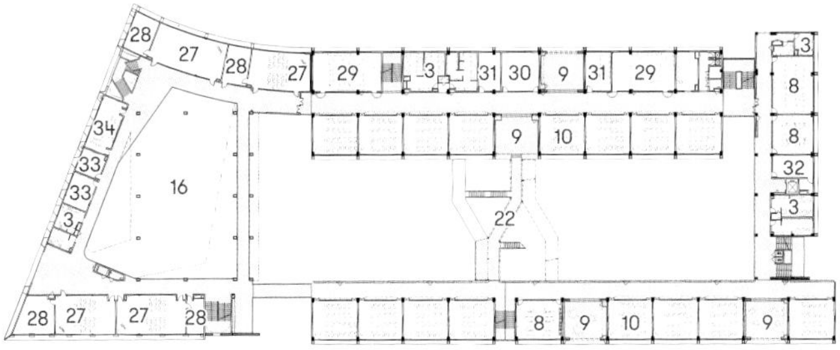

Third-floor plan

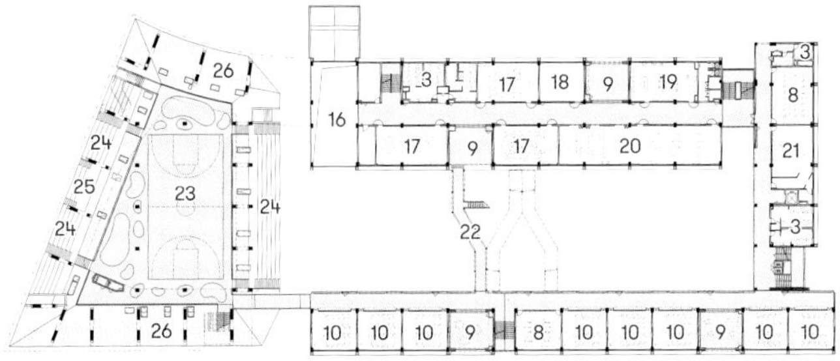

Second-floor plan

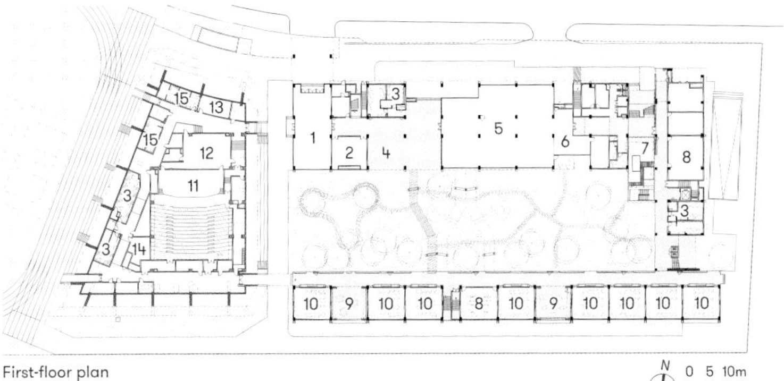

First-floor plan

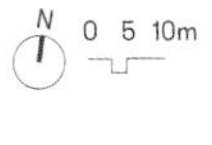

1. Lobby
2. Reception
3. Restroom
4. Semi-outdoor exhibition space
5. Library
6. Teacher's reading room
7. Sunken courtyard
8. Office
9. Common area
10. Classroom
11. Multifunction hall
12. Dance room
13. Physical fitness test room
14. Equipment room
15. Showers and lockers
16. Void
17. Science classroom
18. Speech room
19. Baking classroom
20. Future laboratory
21. Young Pioneers' headquarter
22. Overpass
23. Covered sports field
24. Grandstand
25. Rostrum
26. Grass slope
27. Music classroom
28. Storage for musical instrument
29. Art classroom
30. Activity room
31. Storage for art classroom
32. Meeting room
33. Counseling room
34. Psychology classroom
35. Public classroom
36. Computer classroom
37. Terrace
38. Storage
39. Handiwork classroom
40. Ipad classroom
41. Television studio
42. Multimedia classroom
43. Basketball gymnasium
44. Darts room
45. Auxiliary room
46. Hi-tech activity room
47. Roof garden
48. Lounge
49. Students' activity room
50. Broadcasting room

Façade facing the playground

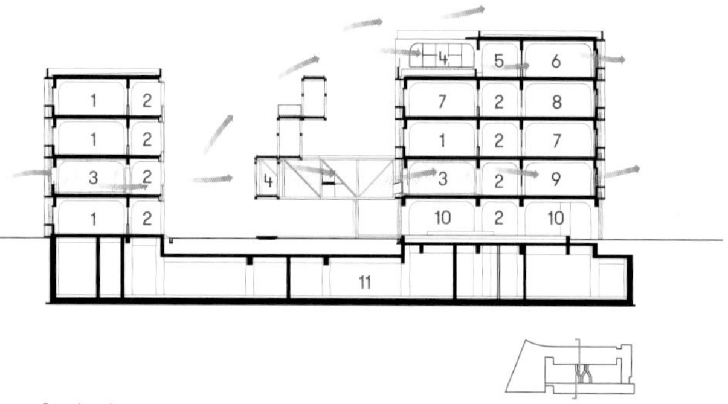

Section 1

1. Classroom
2. Corridor
3. Common area
4. Overpass
5. Roof garden
6. Meeting room
7. Storage for art room
8. Meeting room
9. Handwork classroom
10. Semi-outdoor exhibition area
11. Basement

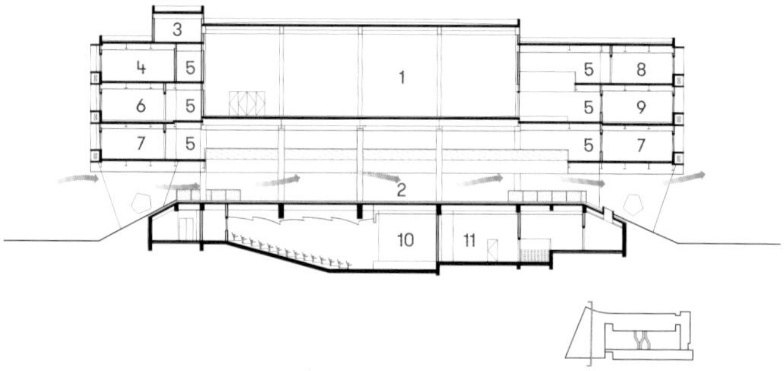

Section 2

1. Basketball gymnasium
2. Covered sports field
3. Equipment room
4. Activity room
5. Corridor
6. Ipad classroom
7. Music classroom
8. Darts room
9. Multimedia classroom
10. Multifunction hall
11. Dance room

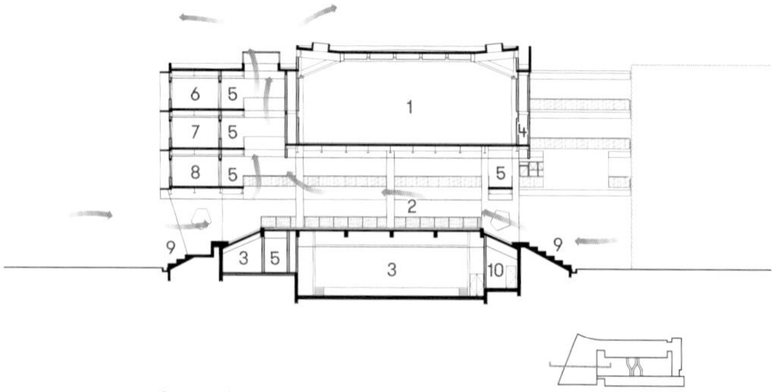

Section 3

1. Basketball gymnasium
2. Covered sports field
3. Multifunction hall
4. Equipment room
5. Corridor
6. Team activity area
7. Television studio
8. Counseling room
9. Grandstand
10. VIP room

0 3 5 10m

Malabar Headquarters

View from the entry bridge

Architect firm: STAPATI
Principal architect: Tony Joseph
Design team: Tony Joseph, Mohandas, Poonam Noufal, Sujith G.S., Kiran, Rajeesh, Likesh K.P.
Location: Calicut, Kerala, India
Area: 18,316 square meters
Completion date: 2018
Photography: Tims Jose Kunnath, Sujith G. S., Sahil

Located in Calicut, in the tropical context of Kerala, India, the Malabar Group headquarters had to contend with a steep sloping site that faced west. The design is thus resolved as a series of levels along the contours, which keeps the intervention on the site to a minimum.

The lower four levels accommodate the parking and service areas, with patterned terra cotta *jaalis* and greenery that define the façade. Office spaces rise up from a large, landscaped podium placed above those lower levels; it also serves as the main entry level. The podium level is accessed through an interestingly designed bridge that is set-off by thoughtfully designed landscaping, which helps create a sense of arrival.

To take advantage of the wonderful views all around, the office areas are designed as transparent open plans and rise up four floors above the podium. Responding to the sloping site, the office spaces are resolved as two separate blocks, with a green landscape spine in between. Strategically placed balconies with large trees and vegetation on the western façade cut out the intense sun, creating a green buffer. They also serve as gardens in the sky, providing spill-out spaces which can be accessed from various floors. Intermittently placed wooden trellises allow climbers to grow and trail, which helps in cutting out the harsh sunlight, along with the double-glazed units on the western façade. The roof is designed as a landscaped gathering space which slopes all the way down to the ground, and has amphitheaters, lounges, pavilions and plenty of vegetation, serving as a space in which colleagues can get together and unwind. The green roof slopes down to the ground on the south to reduce the intensity of the southern sun, also acting as insulation to the office spaces below. Cut-outs in between allow employees to move out onto the green roof.

The interiors express a contemporary design aesthetic with exposed materials like polished concrete flooring and cement board finishes, which contrast with the sleekness of glass and mild steel. Innovatively designed furniture and artworks accentuate the vibrancy of the space. A conscious decision was taken to avoid using a false ceiling, so as to reduce material usage. The services are thus exposed above the eye level and (completely) finished in black, creating a raw industrial aesthetic in the interiors, which is contrasted with the bright colors of the furniture and the artworks.

Natural vegetation is introduced into the interiors through spill-out balconies and the central landscaped spine showcasing dense greenery, providing opportunities for social interactions, thereby promoting the psychological well-being of the employees. The central landscape has a solar screen roof on top to accommodate the energy demands of the building. Rainwater collected on the roof and other surfaces are channeled to percolation pits and help in recharging the ground water. The inherent honesty in the usage of materials, along with the contextually relevant design creates a highly sustainable building—one which is integrally connected to nature.

View of the green buffer from the entrance podium

View of Malabar Group headquarters

Entry to the building at the podium level

Aerial view of Malabar Group headquarters

View from the central landscape spine

The connecting bridges above the landscape spine

The roof is designed as a landscaped gathering space

View of the reception lounge

The executive floor lobby with a view of the distant hills

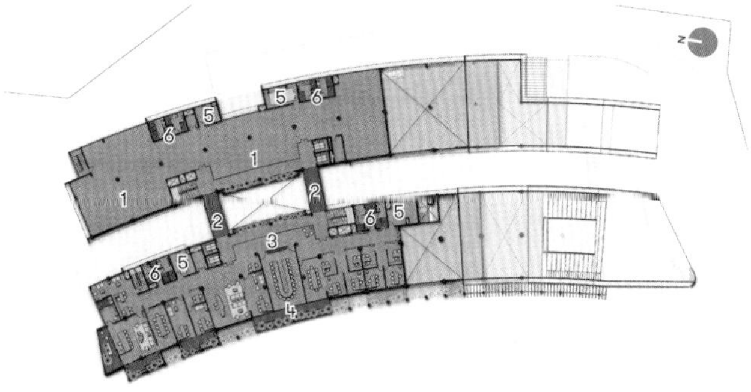

Fourth-floor plan

1. Office space
2. Connecting bridge
3. Executive wing
4. Green buffer
5. Services
6. Restrooms

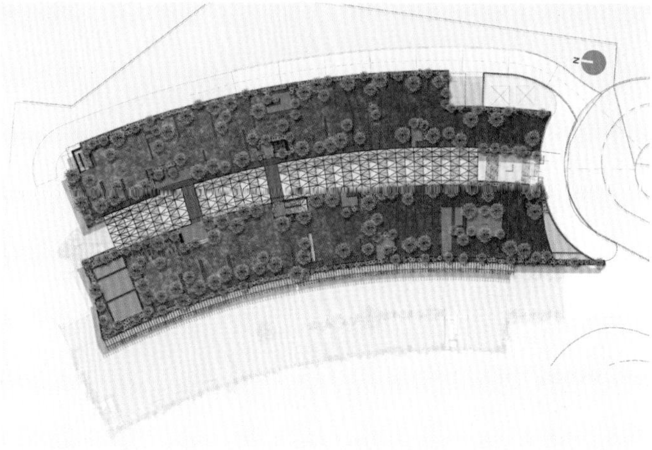

Terrace plan

Second-floor plan

1. Lobby
2. Office space
3. Restrooms
4. Services
5. Open terrace
6. Conecting bridge
7. Green buffer
8. Landscaped terrace

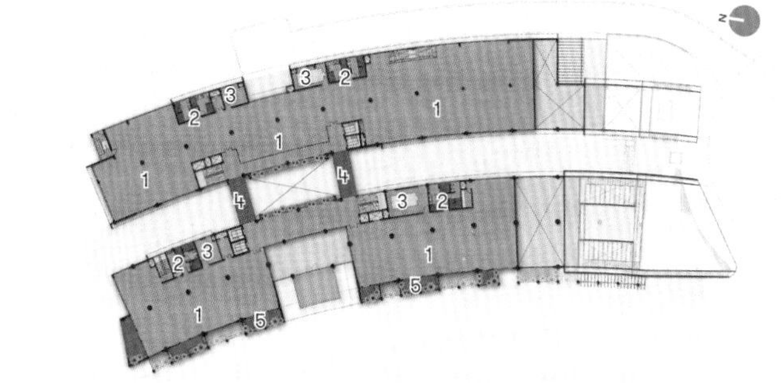

Third-floor plan

1. Office space
2. Restrooms
3. Services
4. Conecting bridge
5. Green buffer

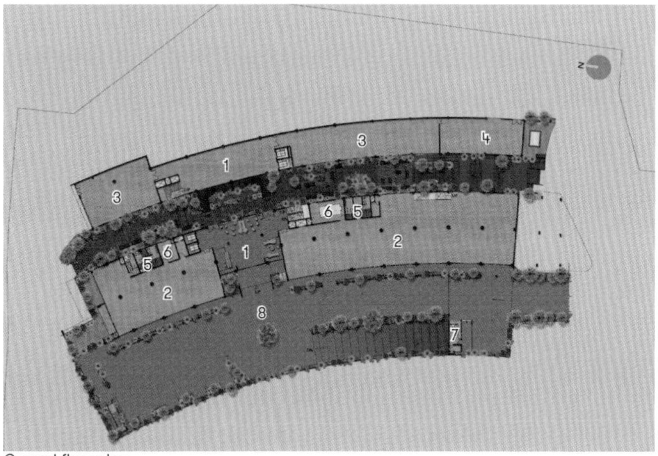

Ground-floor plan

1. Lobby
2. Office space
3. Recreation area
4. Chiller plant room
5. Restrooms
6. Services
7. Security room
8. Podium

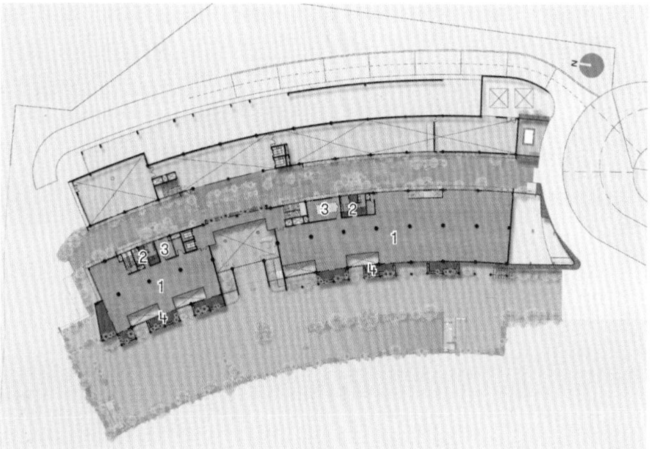

First-floor plan

1. Office space
2. Restrooms
3. Services
4. Green buffer

Gardens in the sky

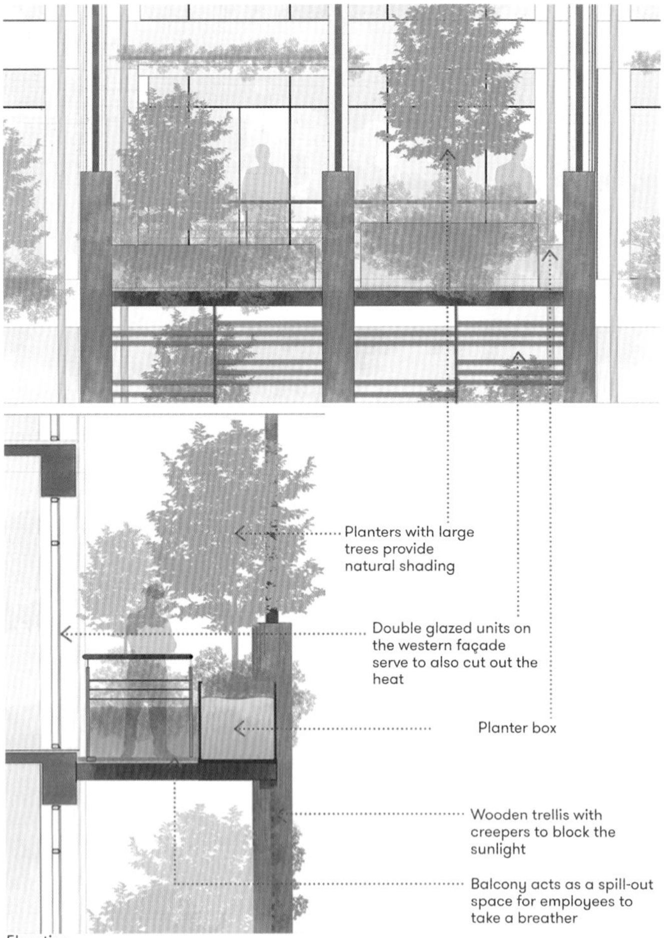

Elevation

West elevation

Section—landscaped spine

Vallabh Bhawan Secretariat

A panoramic view of the Secretariat displays its monumental scale at a single glance

Architect firm: CP Kukreja Architects
Principal architect: Dikshu C. Kukreja
Location: Bhopal, Madhya Pradesh, India
Area: 929,030 square meters
Completion date: 2018
Photography: Kapill Kamra

Vallabh Bhawan is the State Secretariat of Madhya Pradesh and is located atop Arera Hill in Bhopal, Madhya Pradesh, India. Flanked by a large lake on one side of the hill and a refreshing green expanse on the other, the site is blessed with views of the remarkable natural, scenic beauty that the vicinity is known for. These views are framed by an apparent visual axis created by the buildings of Vindhyachal Bhawan and Satpura Bhawan on either side, with an exquisitely landscaped foreground.

The existing context reflects an amalgamation of modern architecture in the buildings of the Secretariat (housed within a built-up area of 929,030 square meters) and traditional *charbagh*-style landscaped gardens[1] commonly seen during the time of the *nawabs* of Madhya Pradesh. Completed within three years, and situated on a site area of 25 acres—at such a strategic location that it can be seen from the far reaches of the city—Vallabh Bhawan was imagined to be the "crowning jewel" of Arera Hill, offering magnificent views to and from Bhopal.

Furthering the strong axial relationship of Vallabh Bhawan with Vindhyachal Bhawan and Satpura Bhawan (where offices of the various departments of Madhya Pradesh's government are housed), on either side within the site, a central promenade extends to the other end, aligning the building with the New Vidhan Sabha (Legislative Assembly). This creates a strong visual relationship between the "legislature" and the "executive," an axis previously unexplored, linking them to an integrated master plan.

Inspired by a modern interpretation of the turrets, horizontal bands, and stepped forms in the architecture around it, Vallabh Bhawan imbibes these contextual influences into its own architectural vocabulary to reflect a seat of power that celebrates the cultural richness of its state, hand-in-hand with contemporary styles.

The planning of Vallabh Bhawan itself rests on a purely rational interrelationship between the various functions of the building, segregated into three distinct program elements within a single, compact, and efficient complex: namely, visitor access zones, staff access zones, and VIP access zones. Some of the facilities provided here include meeting halls, conference halls, ministers' rooms, library, and dispensary. The U-shaped form of the building not only creates an inviting entrance, but also forms a seamless loop between the three primary buildings, creating a strong correlation between them. The design frames views of the site through an interplay of scales and proportions.

Traditional architectural elements like *chhatris* (semi-open, elevated, dome-shaped pavilions), *jaalis*, and colonnades are given a contemporary flavor by using restraint and keeping the forms simple, so that the basic shape may express itself. The sweeping form of the turrets, popularly referred to as the "Beacons of Democracy," are prominently visible from around the city, reaffirming citizens' confidence in a strong and vibrant democratic nation. In addition to this, modern elements such as fins, pergolas, and solar panels keep the structure protected from the harsh sunlight. Landscape strategies involve the use of evergreen trees to obstruct solar heat gain, indigenous plants that require little water, and a zero-discharge rainwater system for maximum water conservation on the site.

The design of Vallabh Bhawan aims to translate the rich cultural fabric of the state and bring it to the global stage using contemporary styles through architecture. This amalgamation of architectural vocabularies, when married together, binds the glory of the past with the aspirations of a forward-looking community to create a unique identity that embodies the spirit of Madhya Pradesh. The building has received wide public acclaim from the local press, hailing it as a trendsetter, while also winning it global recognition.

1. A *charbagh*-style garden usually features a quadrilateral plan, with cross-axial canals centered on a water landscape or pavilion.

An evening perspective shot of Vallabh Bhawan

View of stepped terraces

View of the front porch

1. Multilevel parking
2. Utility block
3. Existing godown
4. Vallabh Bhawan II
5. Vallabh Bhawan I
6. Vallabh Bhawan III
7. Parking

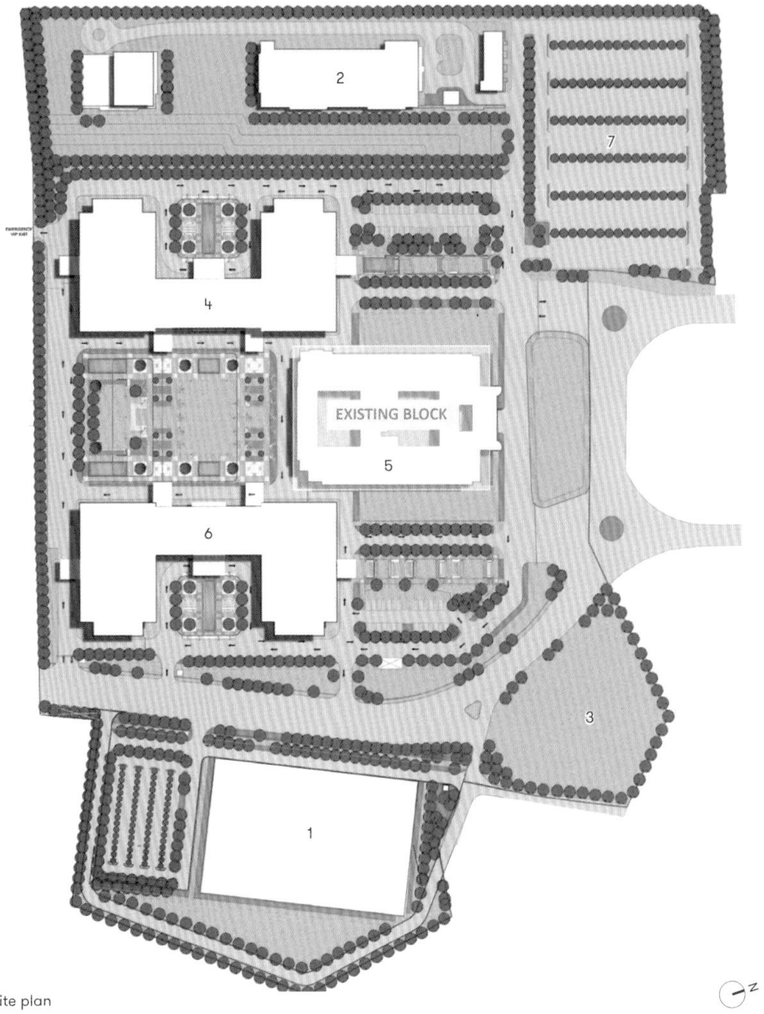

Site plan

A harmonious juxtaposition of modern and natural materials is featured in the design through the use of curtain glazing on natural materials such as sandstone

The entrance opens-up to a spacious reception area which is naturally lit by daylight

View of inner corridors

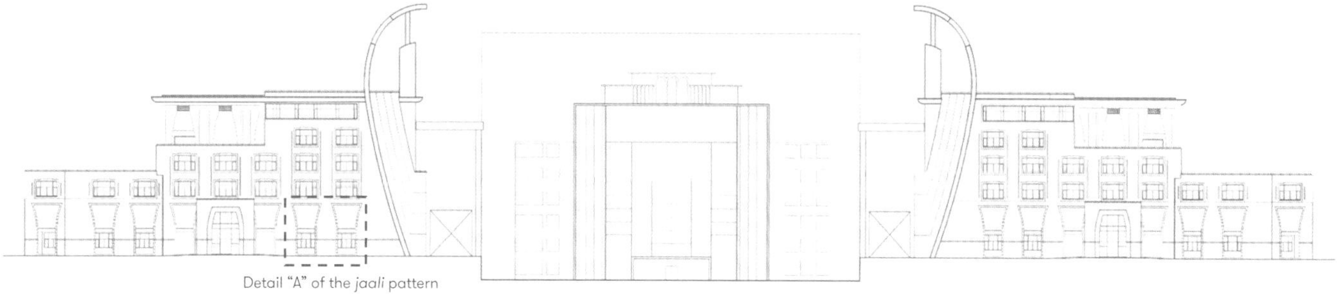

Detail "A" of the *jaali* pattern

Detail "A" of the *jaali* pattern

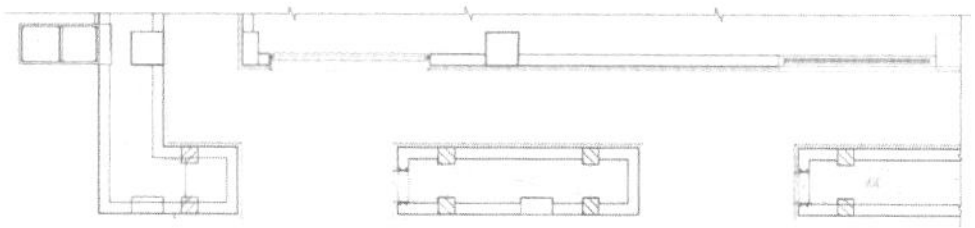

Front elevation of the office block and a detailed part-elevation and section of the office block

The majestic and striking turrets have been called the "Beacons of Democracy"

Attractive shadow patterns created by the *jaali*

Shindagha Historic District

Welcome Pavilion entrance

Architect firm: X Architects
Principal architect: Ahmed Al Ali, Farid Esmaeil
Design team: Ahmed Al Ali, Farid Esmaeil, Mohammad Abu Farha, Sebestiano Baldan, Helene Daher, Brian Walter Abarintos, Luis Martins, Jacky Tang, Yazeed Obeid, Christian Geronimo, Hala Al Juboori, Halla Ibrahim, Reem Helal, Arvin Padayo, Eyad Zarafeh, Imran Rashid, Islam Elsafany, Abdulrehaman Khalid, Haidar Lutfi, Ahmad Mansour
Location: Dubai, United Arab Emirates
Area: Welcome Pavilion—483 square meters; Story of The Creek—1,371 square meters; Perfume House—1,137 square meters
Completion date: 2020
Photography: Fernando Guerra

Al Shindagha historic neighborhood is located on the shore of the Khor Dubai (Dubai Creek in English), Dubai, Unite Arab Emirates, bordered on the south by Bur Dubai, and on the west by Port Rashid. Al Shindagha district began to expand when the Ruler of Dubai, Sheikh Saeed Al Maktoum, settled in the neighborhood from 1912 to 1958.

As part of Dubai's Historical District, along with Deira and Bur Dubai, Al Shindagha is currently undergoing major conservation and renovation work to turn the district into a prominent cultural destination.

The design scope for the renovation initiative of Dubai's Historical District extends across three distinct projects, which include Shindagha Expo 2020 Welcome Pavilion, Story of the Creek, and Perfume House.

The design approach was conceptualized based on Al Shindagha's heritage and context (which was closely studied), and aimed at reviving and restoring the neighborhood's identity in a contemporary setting. Designing a visitor center and museum in a context with many historic layers was a challenging experience that was overcome by creating a coherent synthesis between the old and new. Traditionally, the district's fabric portrayed harmony and the integration between the natural and built environments. The architects conceptualized a design that revisits the past and reinterprets it in an innovative methodology, while remaining rooted in the rich cultural heritage.

The Shindagha Expo 2020 Welcome Pavilion acts as a meeting point and information center for visitors to Dubai's Historical District. Situated between traditional mud houses, the pavilion is designed as an open "plaza" with a roof. Teak wood has been chosen for the construction of this roof, as an acknowledgment of the significant role wooden dhows played in the triumph of Old Dubai. The shifting walls provide the flexibility to contain the space or let it flow out into the surrounding context.

Story of the Creek Museum serves as an introduction to the vibrant history of Dubai and provides visitors with an excellent understanding of the context in which Dubai grew and developed into the thriving metropolis that it is today. It also shows how the city's leaders, both past and present, were essential in providing the vision behind this extraordinary expansion. Visitors will leave the museum with an in-depth understanding of how Dubai Creek has been a generator of trade, wealth, and success.

Perfume House explores Emirati culture via scent and the heritage that stems from its fabrication and use. Visitors will be invited to explore scents via stations that allow them to compare and experiment with the different scents that are unique to Dubai. Scent is an integral part of Emirati hospitality, through which a well-balanced combination of tangible and intangible heritage come together to create a compelling and unique story.

Welcome Pavilion—alley view

Welcome Pavilion—front elevation

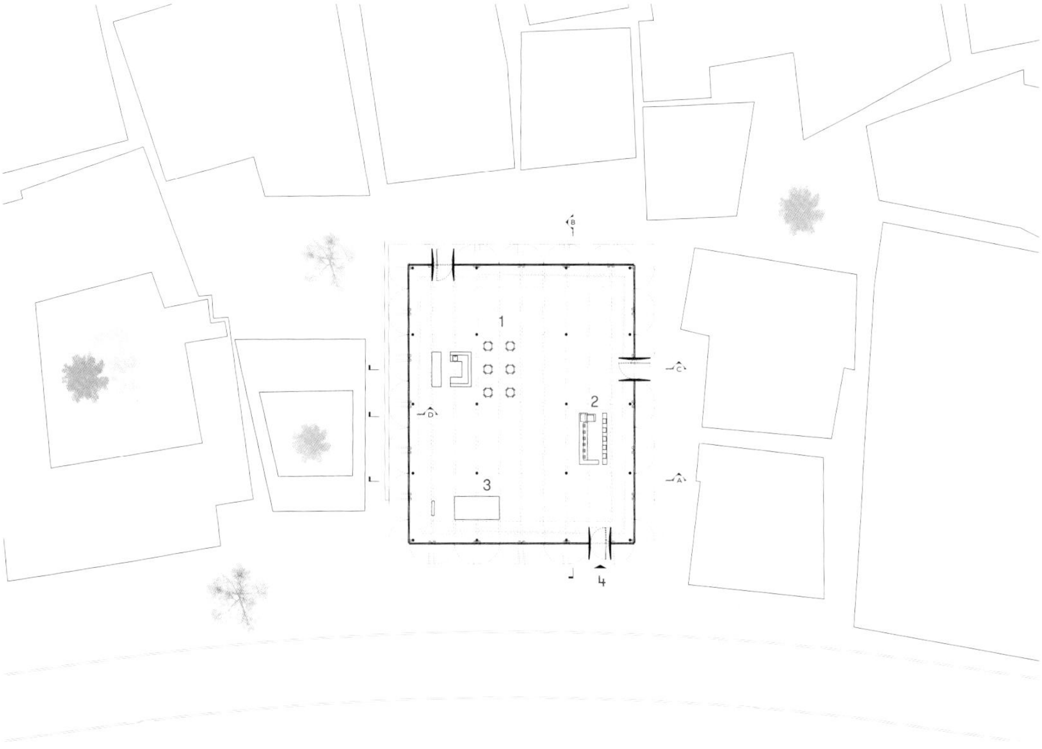

Welcome Pavilion—ground-floor plan

1. Café area
2. Ticketing
3. Model area
4. Entry

Welcome Pavilion roof detail

Welcome Pavilion interior

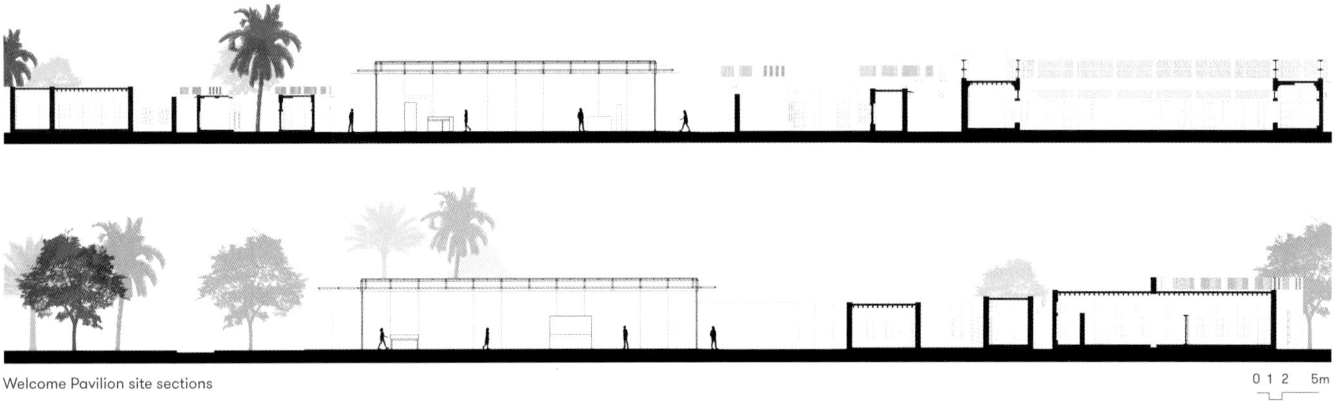

Welcome Pavilion site sections

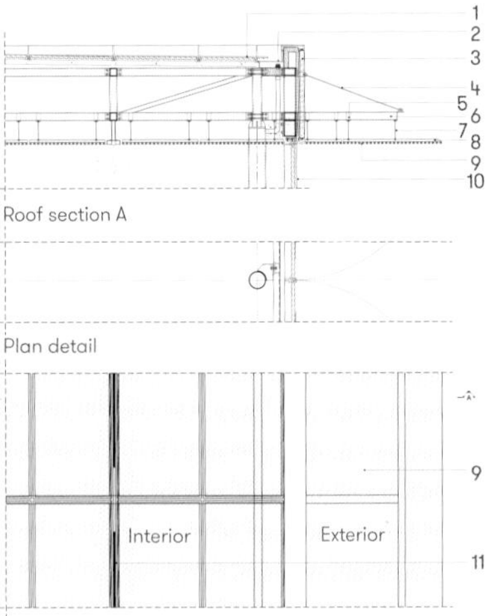

Welcome Pavilion roof detail section

1. Roof glass panel
2. Roof drainage into column
3. Sandwich panel enclosure with insulation
4. Tension cable support
5. Slotted “OMEGA” steel profile
6. 100×100 mm steel tube
7. Threaded steel hangers
8. Slotted “Z” profile steel channel
9. 5×25 mm Areesh teak wood ceiling
10. Fixed window panel
11. Linear light with magnetic track

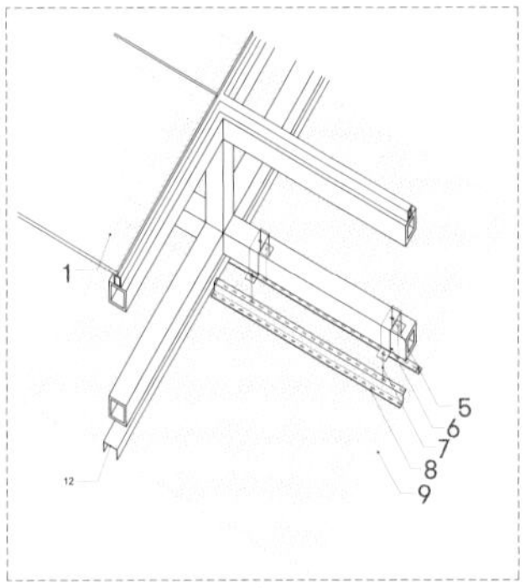

Isometric ceiling detail

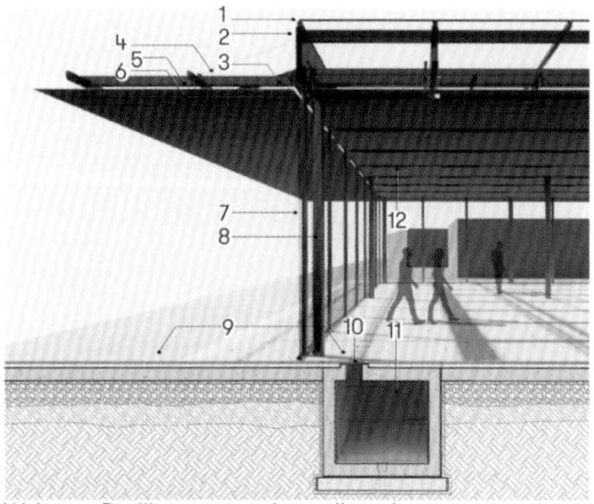

Welcome Pavilion perspective wall section

1. Roof glass panel
2. Steel tube frame for supporting the roof glass
3. 100×100 mm steel tube
4. Tension cable support
5. Threaded steel hangers
6. 25×25 mm Areesh teak wood
7. Operable glass panel
8. Circular steel column
9. Self leveling terrazzo topping on screed
10. Air conditioner steel grating
11. Air conditioner duct trench
12. Linear light

Perfume House interior courtyard

Perfume House interior

Perfume Exhibition at Perfume House

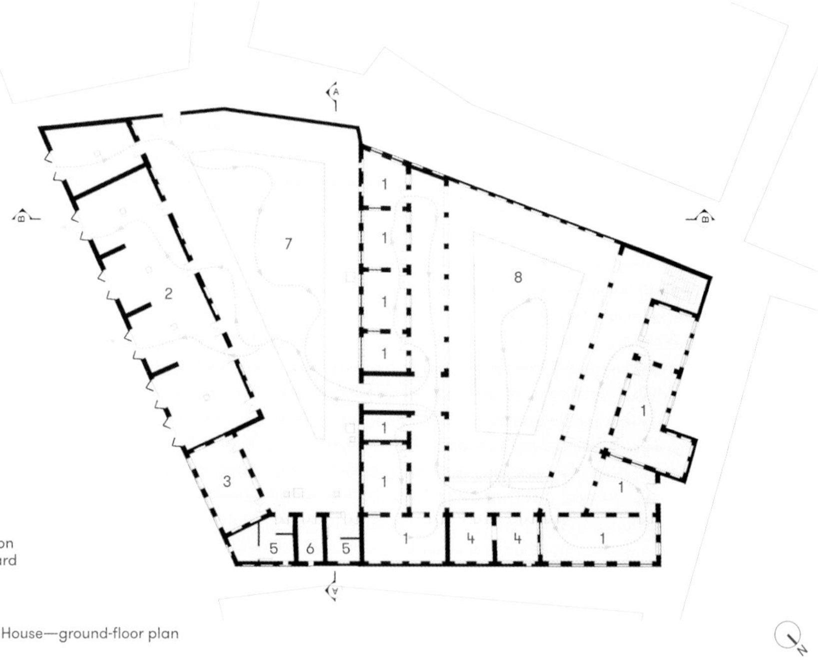

1. Exhibition
2. Retail area
3. Visitor services
4. AV/IT room
5. Restrooms
6. Electrical room
7. Perfume Exhibition
8. Outdoor courtyard

Perfume House—ground-floor plan

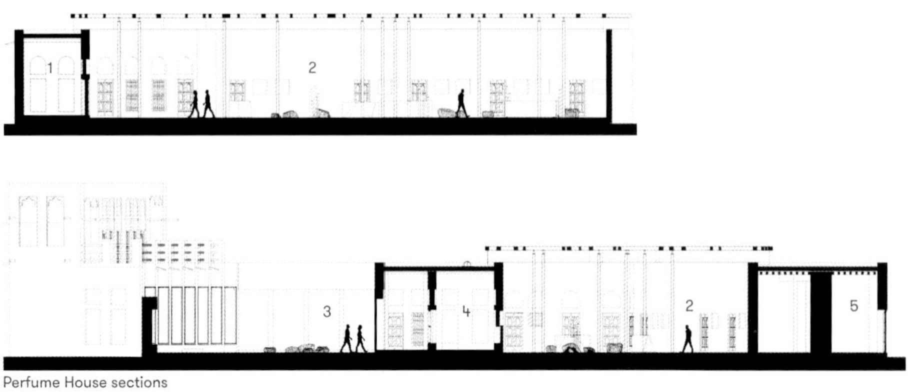

1. Toilet
2. Perfume Exhibition
3. Courtyard
4. Exhibition
5. Retail

Perfume House sections

Story of the Creek interior Exhibition

Mirror exhibition at Story of the Creek

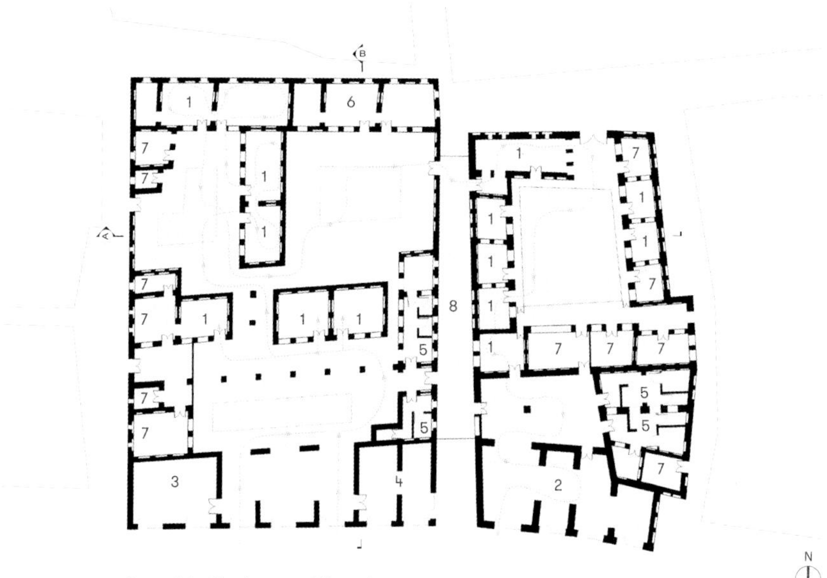

1. Exhibition
2. Retail/café
3. Multipurpose area
4. Visitor services
5. Restrooms
6. Staff
7. Technical/storage
8. Sikka (passage in-between)

Story of the Creek—ground-floor plan

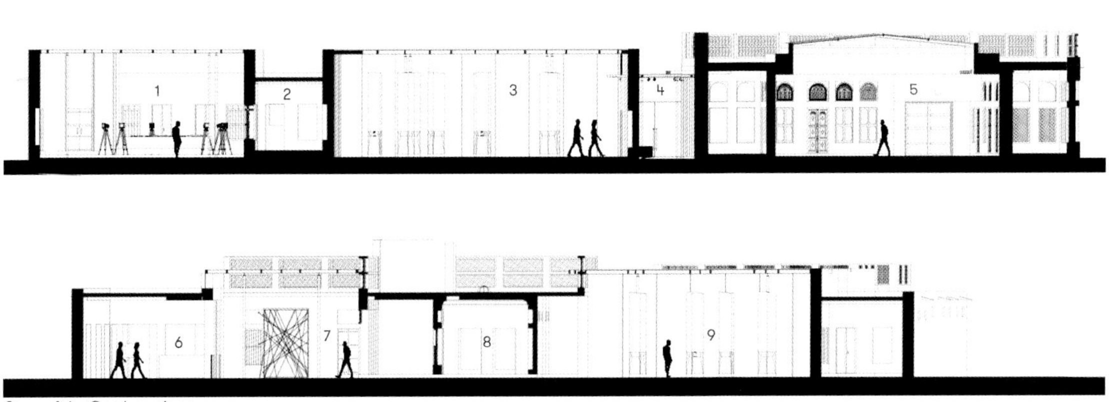

1. Life around the Khor Exhibition
2. The vision of the Leaders Exhibition
3. People of the Khor Exhibition
4. Sikka
5. Multimedia experience
6. Entrance
7. The Khor installation
8. Why people chose the Khor
9. People of the Khor

Story of the Creek sections

Tangshan Quarry Park

Steel grating sidewalk on the bioretention swale

Architect firm: Z+T Landscape Architect
Principal architect: Dong Zhang, Ziying Tang
Design Team: Qing Zhang, Min Xu, Yifan Chen, Shuai Yuan, Yupeng Yang, Xin Liu, Shaohao Bian
Location: Nanjing, China
Area: 40 hectares
Completion date: 2019
Photography: Hai Zhang, Bing Lu

The project is located 30 kilometers from the center of Nanjing City, China, and on the southside of the Tangshan Mountain. The quarry, formerly known as Longquan Quarry, was the largest limestone mine in the region. Fifteen years of mining operation, between 1990 to 2004, left three gigantic craters in the southside of Tangshan Mountain. Since 2017, a team of landscape architects, mountain maintenance engineers, and soil ecologists have been collaborating to rejuvenate the abandoned quarry and the vicinity.

The elevation changes on the site varied from 49 to 250 meters. From west to east, the largest elevation change of the craters was 199 meters; some rock walls on the site were also in danger of falling and collapsing. In the area below the elevation of 91 meters, the terrain was gentle. In this area, human activities were relatively heavy and ecological value and sensitivity were at a low level. The prolonged industrial activities on the site had polluted the water and soil severely, contributing to a high level of heavy metal in the ground water. The soil was heavily compacted and mixed with rocks and muck, which offered a very poor condition for plant growth. The previous mining activities had also damaged the biodiversity of the area. To tackle these issues, the following design solutions were employed:

While taking into account and incorporating the existing terrain and the area's functional regeneration, the rock walls of the quarry craters were repaired selectively and strategically rather than fully. After a detailed evaluation, the rock walls were sorted into two categories: repair and preserve. The preserved rock walls presented impromptu teaching/learning opportunities that offer a close-up view and first-hand experience of the erosion of the mountain caused by mining. After a careful evaluation of the three key factors of the craters—safety, ecological condition, and terrain—two craters were selected for the introduction of human activities.

Water system management: run-off from high points in the mountain was retained in the reservoirs at the bottom of the crater; as the water in the reservoirs moves downstream, the water runs through a bioretention swale. The bioretention swale helps to reduce the run-off, filter out pollutants, and control the passage of the water. The swale is designed as a system with multiple nodes, enabling the detailed management of the water, while increasing the efficiency of filtration.

Locality, low maintenance, and low cost (the 3Ls) are the principles the design is based upon. For example, the design specified reusing crushed stone found on site, which required no processing, as rocks for construction; gabion walls with local stones were used for retaining, erosion control, and to display signage at the entrance; Corten steel was selected as the main material for the cliff walk and the structures at the playground, matching the natural stained color in the rocky craters visually, as well as the industrial background of the site.

Preserve biodiversity: this was carried out through three strategies—control the invasive species, restore the native species, and protect the endangered species.

Over the past five years, the ecological condition in the quarry has improved significantly. The living conditions of the native flora and fauna have also been protected and improved. This project offers an outdoor experience to locals and tourists set on the prongs of recreation and education and has achieved its purposes of restoring the ecology of the site, as well as sustaining the operation of Tangshan Quarry Park financially and socially.

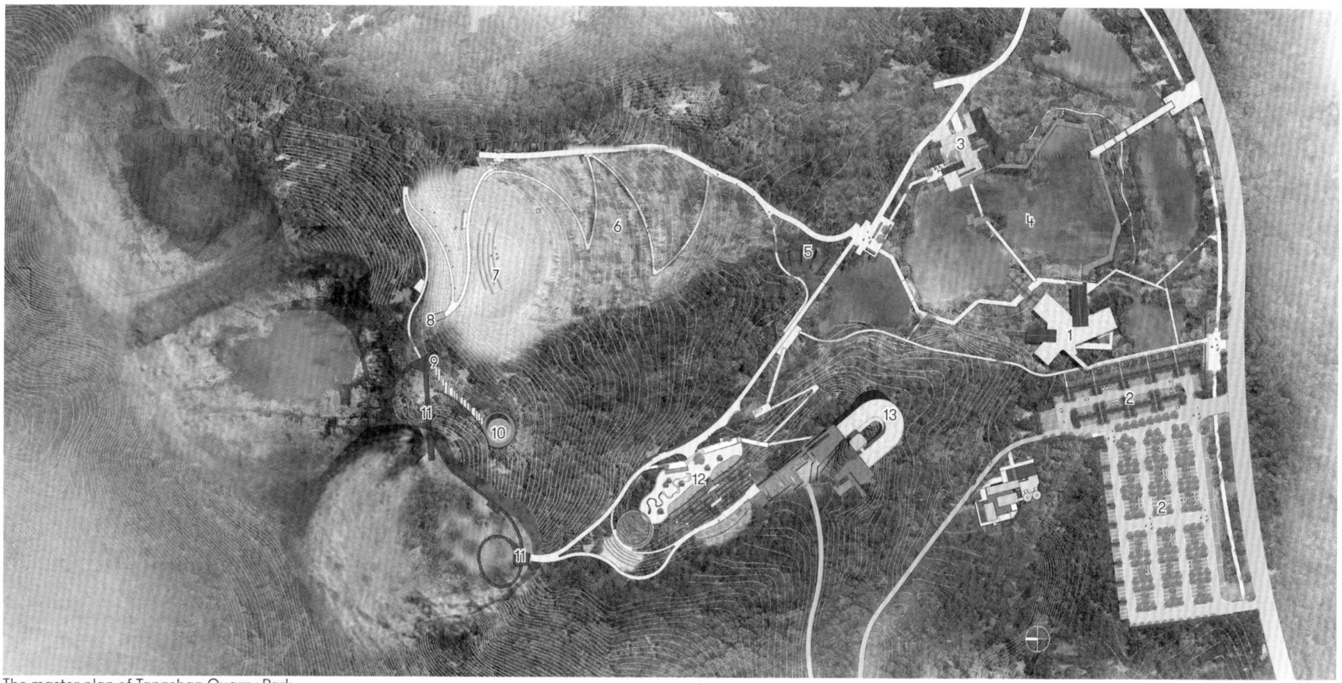

The master plan of Tangshan Quarry Park

1. Visitor Center
2. Parking lot
3. Teahouse
4. Retention pond
5. Rain garden
6. Grass field
7. Amphitheater
8. Tunnel
9. Overlook
10. Pavilion
11. Cliff walk
12. Playground
13 Museum and restaurant

The bioretention swale that collects storm run-off

The "meadow" field

Aerial view of the crater

A variety of mountain-climbing routes along the rocky terrain

The hiking system based on the considerations of the safety, cost, maintenance, and ecological sustainability of the three craters

The sightseeing route offers the opportunity for visitors to access and explore the quarry's rock landscape

The rusty steel route reshapes the façade sequence and corresponds with the rock landscape

The old stockyard was transformed into a playground

The giant trampoline in the playground

The combined entertainment facilities

A range of entertainment facilities entice children

The swings under the Corten steel structure

The circular pavilion

The pavilion offers a vista of the park and city

The pavilion blends into the restored landscape

Alfa Omega School

Bamboo bridge and anteroom from outside

Architect firm: Realrich Architecture Workshop
Principal architect: Realrich Sjarief
Design team: Alifian Kharisma, Miftahuddin Nurdayat, Larasati Ramadhina, Septrio Effendi, Rimba Harendana, Satria Triwardhana, Tatyana Kusumo, Fakhriyyah Khairunnida', Rifandi Septiawan Nugroho, Bambang Priyono
Location: Tangerang, Indonesia
Area: 3,000 square meters
Completion date: 2017
Photography: Eric Dinardi

Alfa Omega School, located in the city of Tangerang, Indonesia, stands on 11,700 square meters of swampland and paddy fields, yet beams bright with local spirit.

The design of the building responds to this unstable soil condition by raising the structure 2.1 meters above the ground. The site was specifically chosen as part of the design scheme, aligned with the goal of bringing children closer to nature through an outdoor learning experience. The building integrates four modular buildings with an efficient access point in one central courtyard to accommodate local land zoning limitations as to what can and cannot be built.

To answer the project brief, the design solution creates optimal collaborations or bridge relationships in the economics of the projects and the creative process of construction—for example, the creative decision of employing a steel and bamboo construction helps extend the project's and materials' economic reach.

Steel structures are selected not only for their ability to effectively withstand structural loads, but also for their construction speed and durability. The whole building is based on this framework, from the foundation to the roof component. Steel, in its variation from thickness to treatments, opens chances for versatile details of design, while bamboo is a flexible material that requires little maintenance in the long-term; it is also readily available within the area. This availability also extends to brick and concrete.

The structure utilizes bamboo for the roof to create a parabolic shape, which enhances the character of Nipah, a type of palm that can be tilted or bent. Using bamboo also helped keep the overall cost of the project low. The brick is stacked in a solid void pattern to allow cross-air circulation through the façade. Meanwhile, polished bare concrete is used as a floor finish, given its durability to withstand the daily traverses of feet.

The school is designed with passive cooling that relies on natural cross-ventilation in its construction—such as the high, exposed ceiling that has been designed as an air passage, and the porous, solid-void bricks on each side of the classroom wall. This allows optimal air circulation within the building, without the need for air conditioning.

To overcome instances of strong sunlight, the structure above the corridor has been cantilevered by 2 meters to create natural blinds (by way of construction) and also offer protection from heavy rains. The Nipah roof, solid brick façade, bamboo ceilings, and concrete floor coverings provide low thermal conductivity that allows the building to have an average temperature of 27 degrees Celsius. The openings in the building have also been designed to allow it to function on one hundred percent daylight during the day; at night, LED lights illuminate the interior.

The project also aims to create collaborative bonds between people and buildings through social cycles, with the involvement of local people—such as employing local craftspeople for the construction of the project. As a bonus, doing so also addressed three other challenges: optimal resources, time constraint, and manpower. Material resources were found within five kilometers of the site, which helped accelerate development while reducing the project's carbon footprint. Beyond local help, the project was also completed by steel welders and bamboo craftspeople from Sumedang, who brought with them their own originality and approaches, giving the end result a feel of layered aesthetics.

The craftspeople were categorized into two types: "light structure," who focused on the roof, and "heavy structure," who were steel and masonry craftspeople focussing on constructing the modular classrooms. The roof has been built with a light triangular steel frame of 600 millimeters by forty craftspeople from Sumedang. The use of inexpensive materials like Nipah and bamboo reduced the initial budget by thirty percent. In the first two months, the "light structure" craftspeople built the piers and roof and ceiling details, which were then joined by heavy structural parts.

View of building from corner

View of building from outside

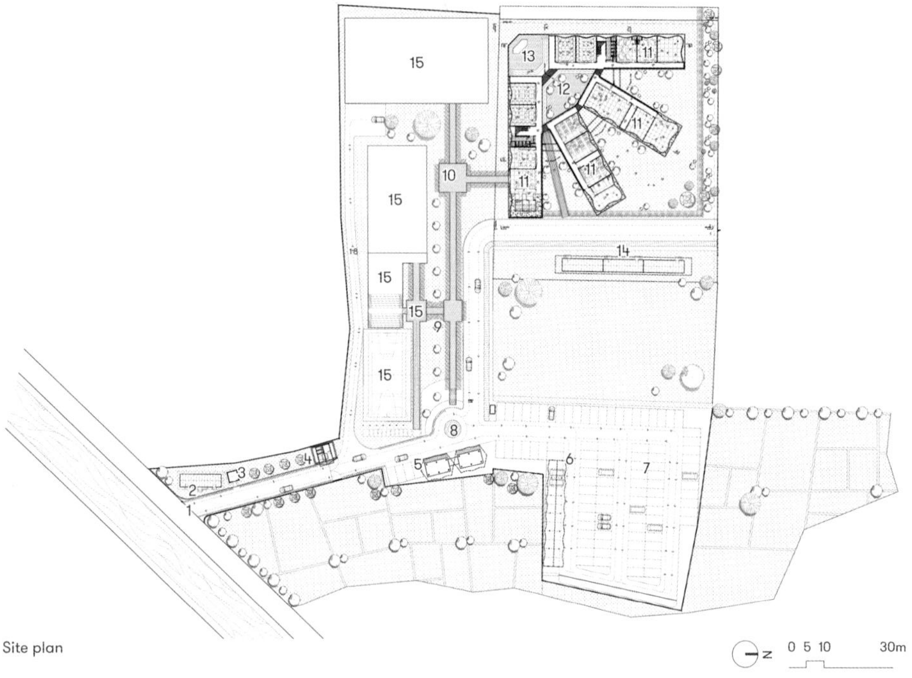

Site plan

1. Entrance
2. Guard office
3. Trash collection/disposal
4. Guard post
5. Clinic and pick-up area
6. Bus parking
7. Car parking
8. Sundial
9. Bamboo bridge
10. Bamboo anteroom
11. Main buildings
12. Inner court
13. Ampitheater
14. Room maintenance
15. Future development area

Exterior view of the restroom from the west

The completed structures and a new one under construction

Workshop building—view from inside

Inner courtyard

Bamboo ramp and bridge

View from the interior courtyard

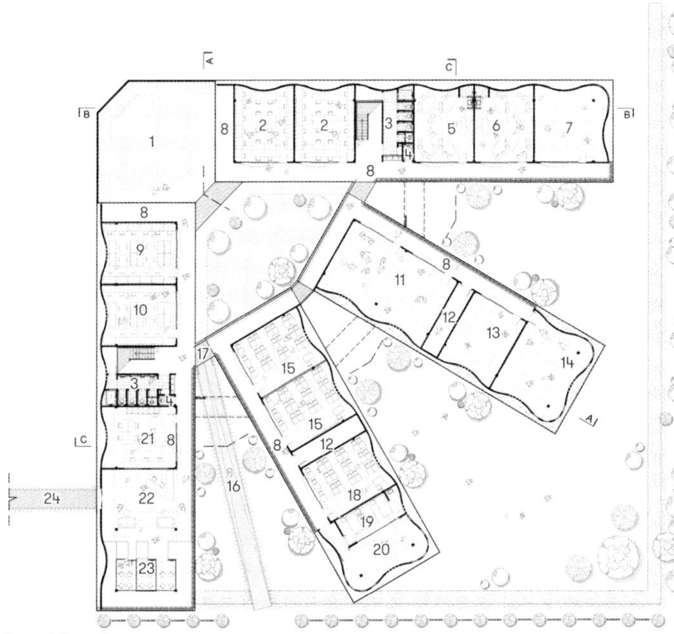

Ground-floor plan

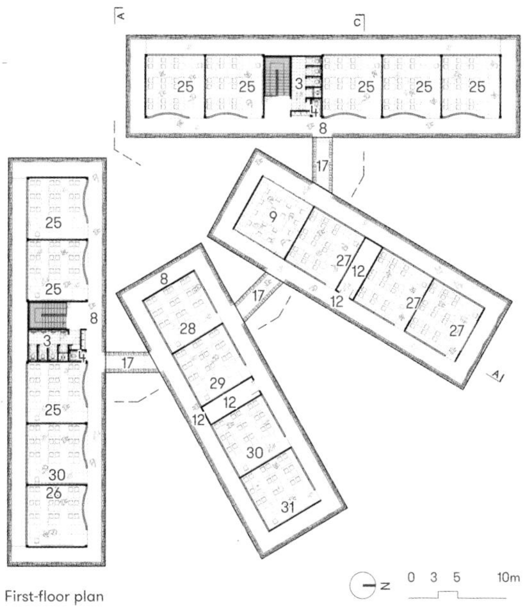

First-floor plan

1. Amphitheater
2. Foundation room
3. Restrooms
4. Staff restrooms
5. Science laboratory of junior high school
6. Science laboratory of senior high school
7. IT laboratory of junior and senior high schools
8. Corridor
9. Teachers' room—kindergarten and elementary school
10. Headmaster's room—elementary school and junior and senior high school
11. R. Serbaguna SMP SMA—multifunction room of junior and senior high school
12. Warehouse
13. Music room—junior and senior high school
14. Library
15. Kindergarten
16. Bamboo ramp
17. Bridge
18. Playgroup area
19. Healthcare room
20. Daycare
21. Administration office
22. Lobby
23. Consultation room
24. Entrance
25. Moving class
26. Religion room—junior high school
27. Classroom
28. Maths room—junior and senior high school
29. Religion room—senior high school
30. Biology room—senior high school
31. Social Sciences room—junior and senior high school

View of building and bamboo ramp from the ground floor

Classroom

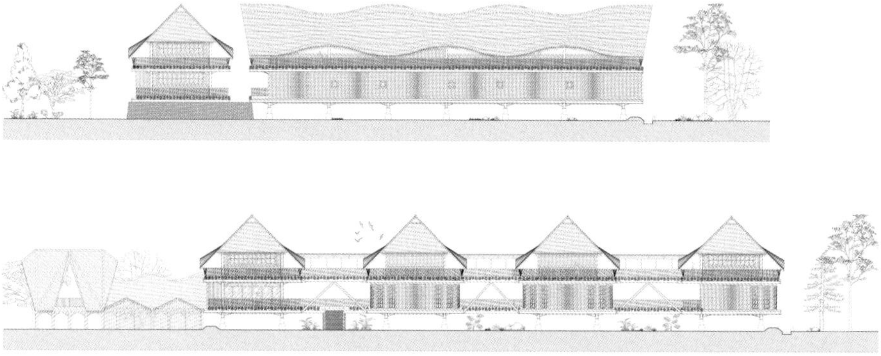

Elevations

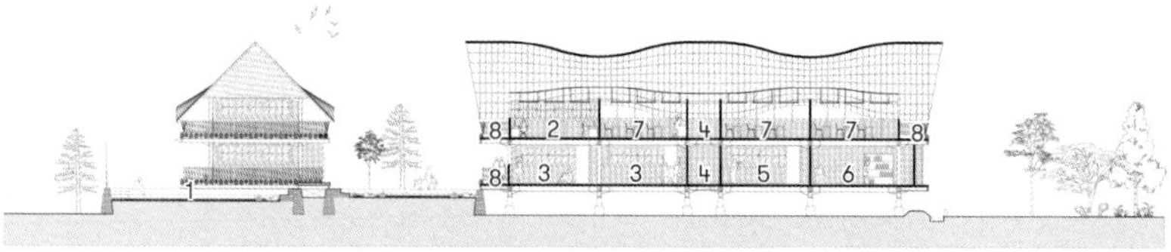

SECTION A

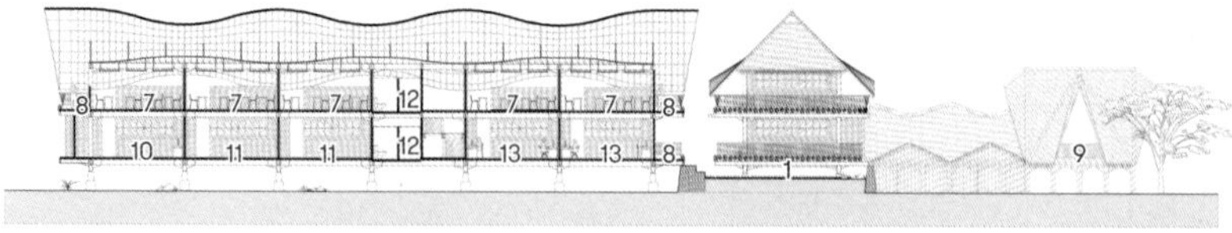

SECTION B

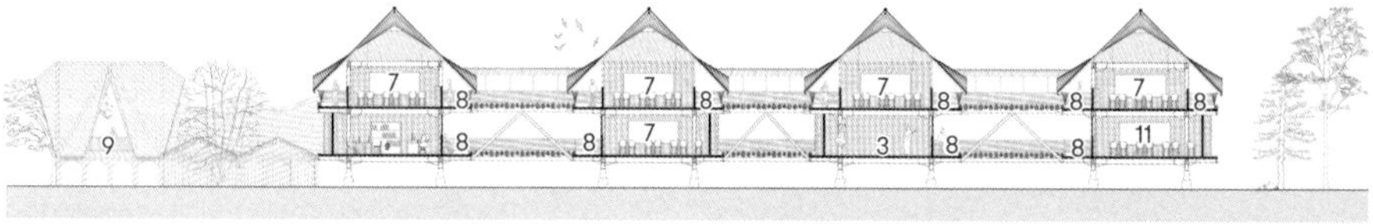

Sections

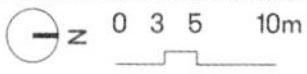

1. Ampitheater
2. Teachers' room
3. Multifunction room
4. Warehouse
5. Music room
6. Library
7. Classroom
8. Corridor
9. Bamboo anteroom
10. IT laboratory
11. Science laboratory
12. Restrooms
13. Foundation room

Curved brick wall

Bamboo bridge and anteroom view from outside

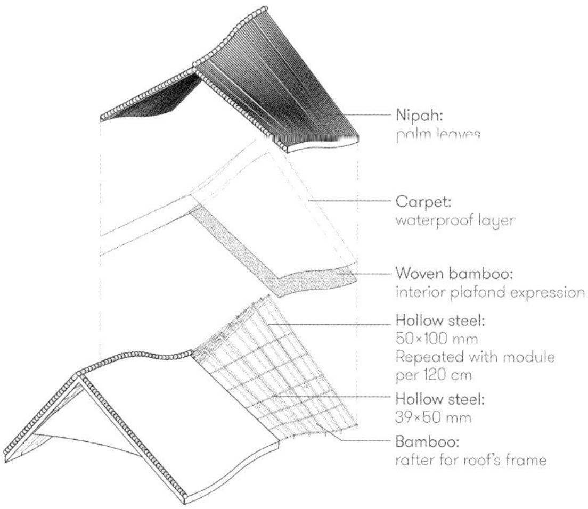

Nipah rooftop detail

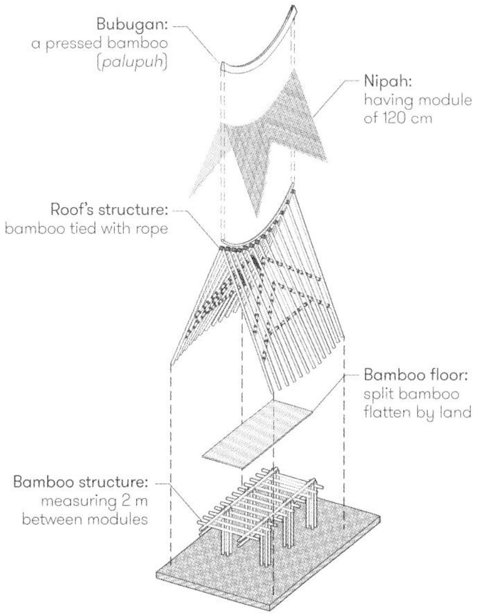

Bamboo bridge detail

Bamboo anteroom bridge

Bamboo ramp view from second-floor corridor

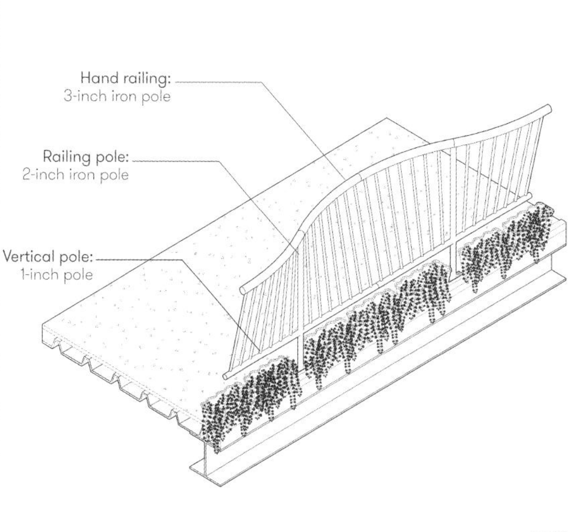

Curved railing detail

Hoshino Resorts KAI Poroto

View from the lakeside

Architect firm: Hiroshi Nakamura & NAP
Principal architect: Hiroshi Nakamura
Design team: (former staff) Taisuke Ishibashi, Kohei Taniguchi, Eizaburo Suzuki; Sadaharu Aoto, Takumi Shido
Location: Hokkaido, Japan
Area: 2,021.37 square meters
Completion date: 2021
Photography: Koji Fujii/TOREAL, Ben Richards

The town of Shiraoi in Iburi, Hokkaido, Japan, which embraces Lake Poroto, is one of the regions where many Ainu (indigenous people of northern Japan) settlements thrived. On the opposite shore, Kotan, a traditional Ainu village, extends out as one of the outdoor exhibits of the National Ainu Museum, with Mount Tarumae in the distance completing the scenery. Through this project, the architects sought to develop a hot spring inn (*ryokan*) that would reflect the Ainu culture while making the most of the natural views.

The *mem*, a kind of hot spring, is important in the Ainu culture and lifestyle, given their daily use of it; even in winter it does not freeze over. The source of Lake Poroto is a *mem* just a few kilometers away. There is another *mem* one on the side of the parking lot of the project site. Therefore, the design team decided to draw the lake water into the site to create a modeled landscape of the Lake Poroto basin. The approach from the parking lot follows the route the Ainu once traveled along the stream from the *mem* to the lake.

On the lakeside, where the guestroom building bridges over the river, a sunken lounge is placed close to the water, such that the canoe dock and ice-free water surface can be viewed while sitting around an open hearth in the lounge.

Guestrooms have a lounge space around a low table in the shape of a hearth, with gentle, indirect lighting, honoring the Ainu family custom of conversing around the hearth of the *chise* (home). Ainu art patterns and designs are incorporated in various ways, such as in the wallpaper, cushion covers, and artworks around the inn, so guests can get a sense of the Ainu, whose lives were very much surrounded by apparel and home décor items embellished with their traditional patterns.

The Sankaku-no-Yu (triangular bath) was inspired by a *kucha*, a temporary hut used by the Ainu as a bivouac when hunting for bears or waiting for salmon in the mountains. The *kucha* has a quiet presence, nestled close to the surroundings without intruding on the beautiful nature around. The *kucha* is based on the Ainu's *ketunni* tripod architecture, which is made of three logs that are connected on the sides. Its distinctive feature is the inverted triangular pyramid apex, with the end of the logs protruding out, which serves as a smoke exhaust and skylight. By turning this into a design element, the hot spring bathhouse with limited windows becomes an ecological structure that gets a gentle and uniform shower of natural light, as well as a natural exhaust of warm humid air via an updraft. When viewed from the guestrooms, the cone-shaped huts blowing smoke from the apex becomes a part of the scenery without disturbing the horizon of the lake.

Since no views could be provided in the Maru-no-Yu (round bath) bathhouse for the locals, it is designed as a cave with an underground hot spring. The skylight has no glass and warm air is carried out naturally, while rain or snow falls inside. The hot spring is a black moor spring that contains organic substances from plants, and reflects the light from the skylight on the water surface. This encourages the behavior of intuitively raising the line of sight upward in search of the light source.

Indigenous trees were planted along the vacant development site, along with white birch, which is regarded as a mother tree that germinates before others, even on desolate land, restoring the forest while protecting other vegetations. A forest of white birch was created by selectively thinning trees on the exterior and inside the hotel, carrying with it the message of protecting and nurturing not only the development site itself, but also the Ainu culture. Through this design intervention, the resort honors the Ainu culture and seeks to restore the profound relationship the Ainu people once had with the forests and rivers.

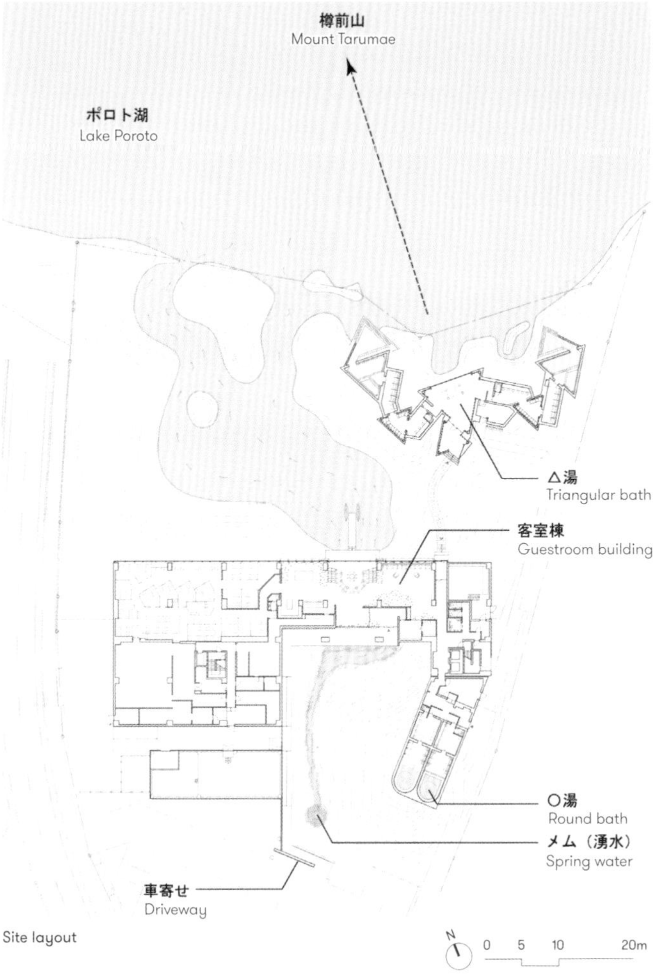

Site layout

View from the resort

View from lakeside

Entrance approach

Library

Entrance

Bath lounge of Sankaku-no-Yu (triangular bath)

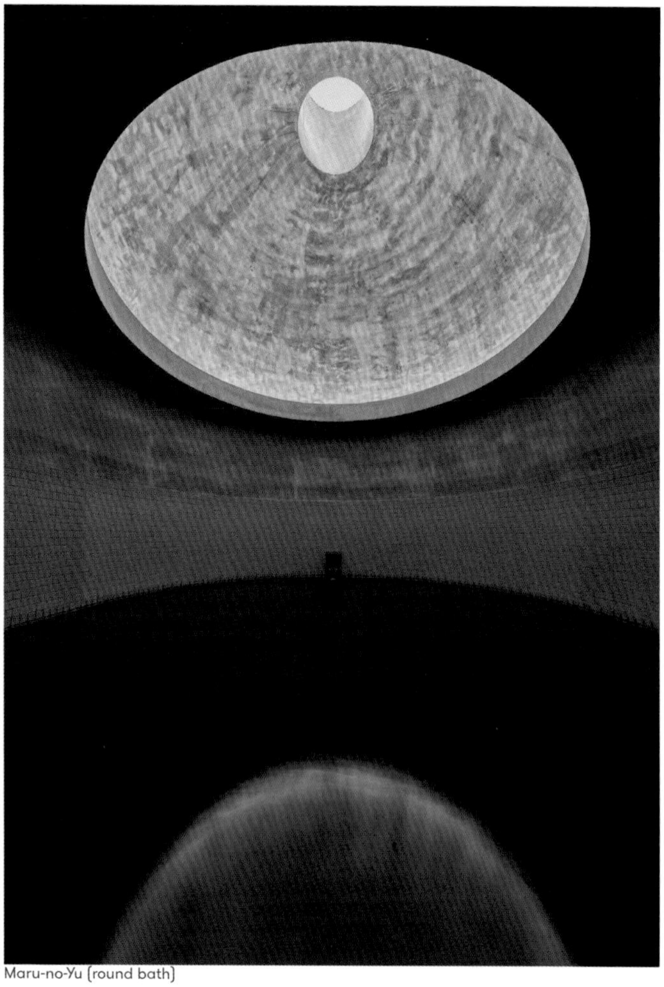
Maru-no-Yu (round bath)

Sunken lounge

Suite with outdoor bath

Guestroom with outdoor bath

Bewboc House

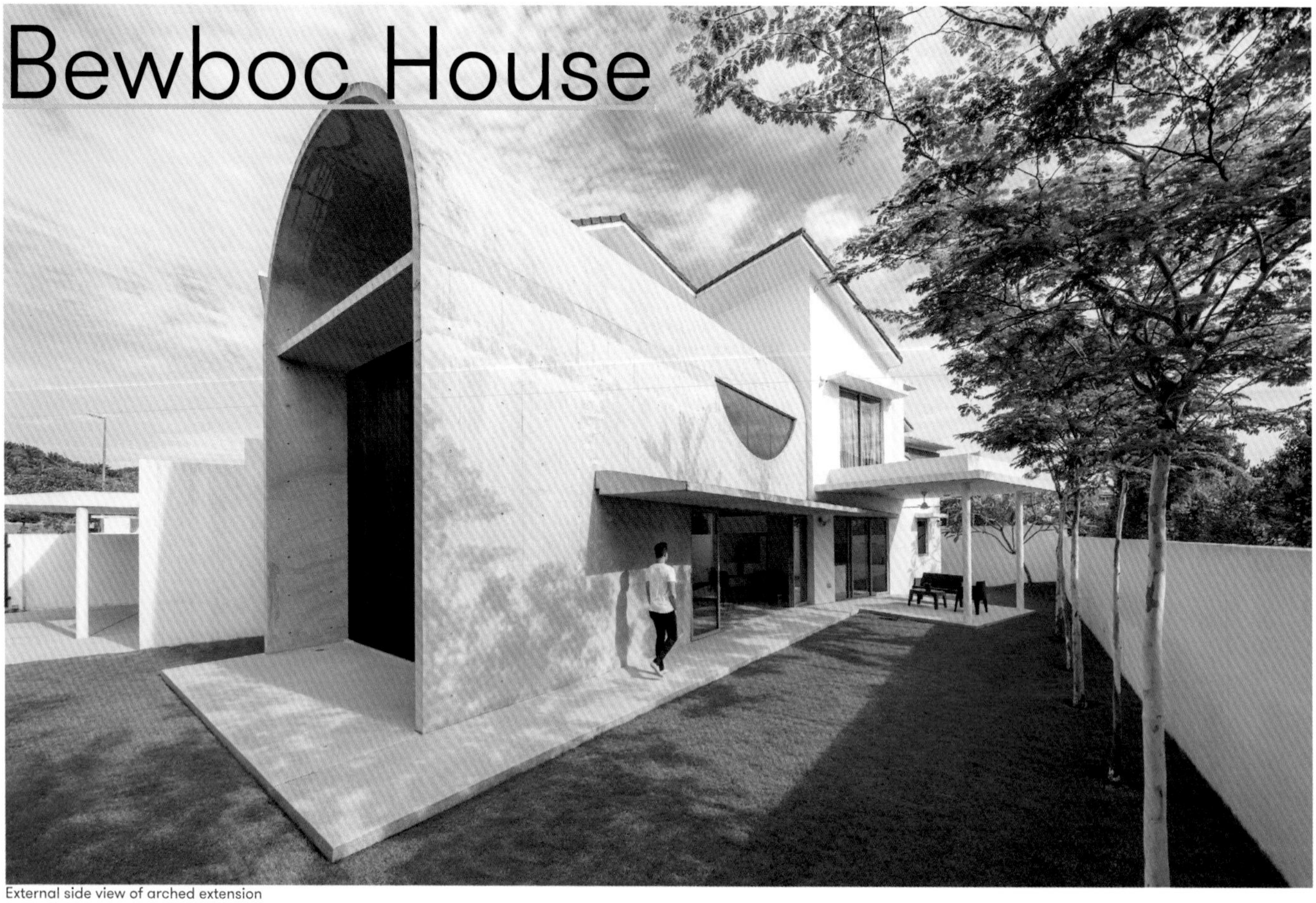
External side view of arched extension

Architect firm: Fabian Tan Architect
Principal architect: Fabian Tan
Location: Kuala Lumpur, Malaysia
Area: 344 square meters
Completion date: 2019
Photography: Ceavs Chua

This suburban terraced house in Kuala Lumpur (KL), Malaysia, is a beautiful example of a minimalistic, yet striking architecture. Based on a project brief that stipulated minimal intervention on the site, the design reimagines the form of this corner house while repurposing the living spaces on the ground level.

The new form is simple yet bold, creating a stark contrast with the existing surrounding tropical suburban homes. As living spaces were orientated parallel to the site boundary, it resulted in a "break" between the original and the new spaces. The triangulated "break" acts as a secure and ventilated lightwell that cools both sides naturally. An arch roof extends outward, creating a vaulted annex that forms the living spaces. The space appears continuous, through the extension of the arch, and is further exaggerated by the materiality of the concrete finish from floor to ceiling. The extension is enhanced by two large doors that open to the garden, providing an uninterrupted connection between the interior and the nature outside.

On the upper floor, the design sets up a dramatic background with a play of curves and levels; the spaces are layered, creating a space hierarchy. The study overlooks the living spaces; adjacent to it is a step-up platform corner for lounging. Behind this is a bedroom overlooking these spaces. The main bedroom connects through a bridge to the outermost floor section of the annex and an open balcony.

To counterbalance the heaviness of the concrete vault, openings were carefully carved out on the upper level. The inverted arch window at the side of the vault is drawn as a continuous "S" when it meets the front arched opening. Walking through the upper levels, this continuity echoes throughout the spaces as lines of openings and points where arches meet. Consequently, this rhythmic play of lines within a heavy structure also lends to a play of light in subtle ways. It's reminiscent of a journey through a cave, perhaps to see the light at the end of the tunnel. This was inspired by the architect's experience of the nature of Gunung Mulu National Park in Sarawak, Malaysia.

Overall, the design of this suburban terraced house is an ideal blend of minimalism and boldness. It creates a striking contrast within the tropical fabric of the surrounding suburban homes, while still keeping its living spaces functional and comfortable for the young family who owns it. The use of materials, the play of curves and levels, and the interplay between light and shadow are elements that make this house unique and memorable.

View from balcony

View of arched structure from entrance

Street view of arched extension

Flowing spaces between the inside and outside

Looking out to the garden from the living room

Scale of door in living space

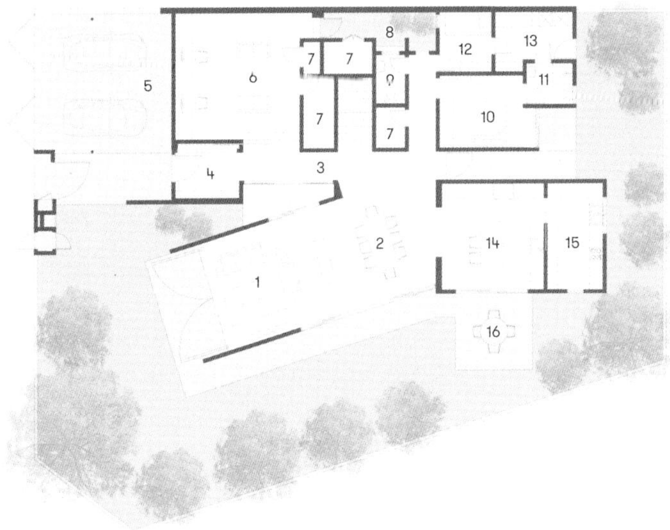

Ground-floor plan

1. Living room
2. Dining room
3. Corridor
4. Foyer
5. Car porch
6. Study/studio
7. Store
8. Air well
9. Powder room
10. Guest bathroom
11. Guest bedroom
12. Utility room
13. Laundry
14. Dry kitchen
15. Wet kitchen
16. Patio

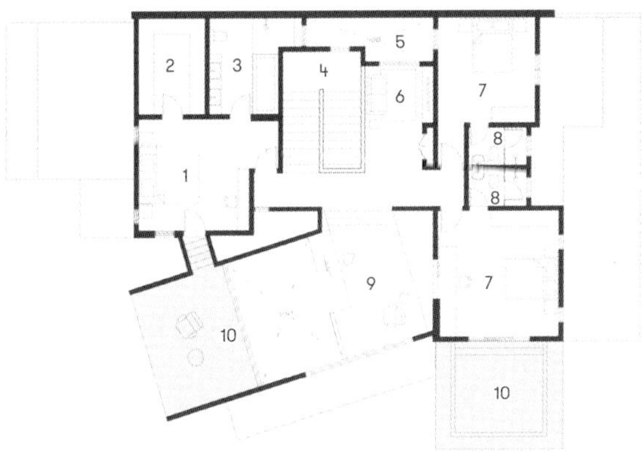

First-floor plan

N 0 1 3 5m

1. Master bedroom
2. Walk-in wardrobe
3. Master bathroom
4. Stairs
5. Air well
6. Family room
7. Bedroom
8. Bathroom
9. Lounge
10. Balcony

View of the interconnection of the spaces on both levels

The space connecting the room and study

View of study

Continuous curves of the interior space

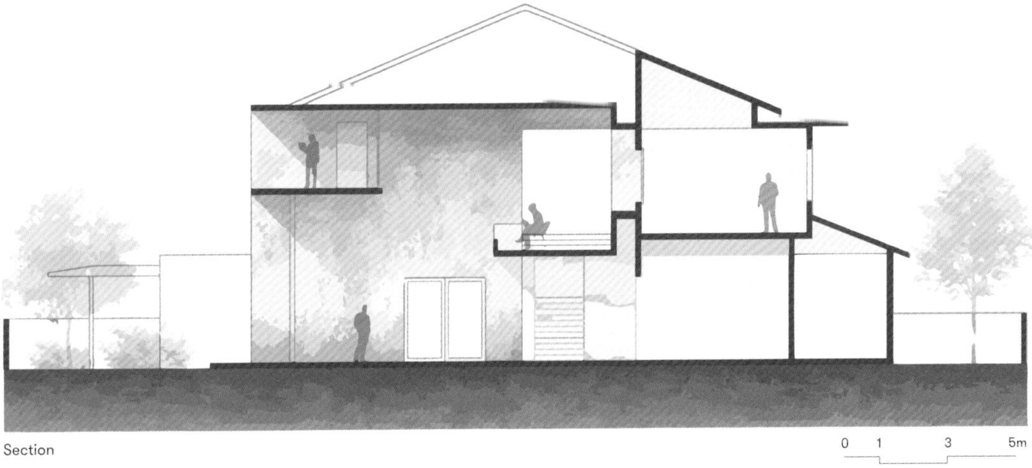

Section

View of interior living spaces at dusk

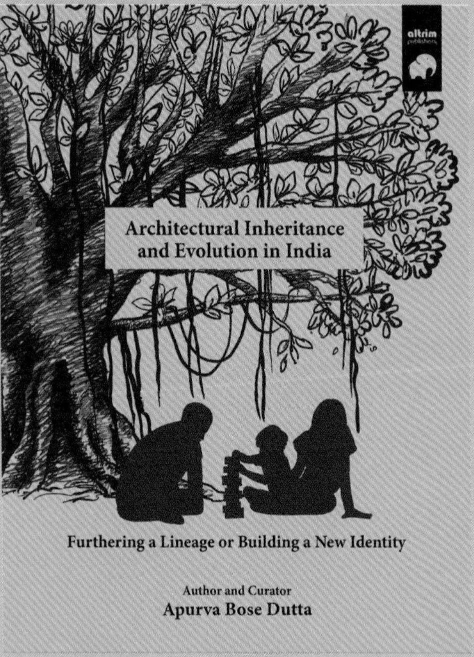

Architectural Inheritance and Evolution in India

Furthering a Lineage or Building a New Identity

Author and curator: Ar. Apurva Bose Dutta

Indian author, award-winning architectural journalist, curator, editor, and educator Ar. Apurva Bose Dutta (www.apurvabose.com) has recently launched her second book, ***Architectural Inheritance and Evolution in India***. Apurva works at the intersection of architectural design writing, thinking, discourse, curation, journalism, criticism, and communications, and is an advisory board member of *Architecture Asia*. Through the narratives of ten acclaimed architectural families in India, her book examines the overlaps of families and architecture in India, a nation that rejoices in its rich family culture and ethos.

The featured families include architects whose contribution to architecture spans many decades: *Sumit Ghosh and Family* (New Delhi), *Uttam C. Jain and family* (Mumbai), *Kembhavis* (Karnataka), *Shahs and Khannas* (Gurgaon, Mumbai, and Vancouver), *Khans* (Nagpur and Gujarat), *Kanvindes* (New Delhi), *Puris* (Mumbai), *S. D. Sharma and Family* (Chandigarh), *Zacharias* (Kerala and Bengaluru), and *Shahs and Gores* (Mumbai).

Traversing the families' individual and collective perspectives, journeys, philosophies, and contributions, the book celebrates architecture across generations, and explores its evolution in India and worldwide through inter-generational narratives. Professor Krishna Rao Jaisim, a prominent architect, patron, and philosopher from India, writes in the book's foreword: "The author highlights the concept of 'Diversity in Unity' rather than 'Unity in Diversity,' where a family encourages competition within rather than be pushed about by external influences, and provides an opportunity without fear of financial failure."

The book is a product of the author's intensive research and detailed conversations with forty members of the ten featured families. An analytical epilogue ties up all the families, investigates how professional and personal attributes can impact interpersonal equations, and highlights how architecture impacts familial bonds. The essays in the book are supported by images of the familys' journeys in architecture.

The book is published by Altrim Publishers and supported by the Council of Architecture of India. For more information on the book, please visit www.apurvabose.com/book-architectural-inheritance-and-evolution-in-india/.

TONGJI ARCHITECTURAL DESIGN (GROUP) CO., LTD.

Exterior of the TJAD office building

ABOUT TJAD

Tongji Architectural Design (Group) Co., Ltd. (TJAD), formerly known as the Architectural Design and Research Institute of Tongji University, was founded in 1958 and has now developed into a well-known large-scale design and consulting group.

Shanghai Museum East Hall

With almost seventy years of history behind it, and with the profound cultural foundation of Tongji University, TJAD has accumulated a rich experience in both engineering design and technical consultancy, progressing notably over the last sixty-four years. TJAD is a design institution with one of the most extensive design qualifications in China, with a business scope that includes consulting, engineering design, project management, geotechnical engineering, and geological exploration in the fields of building engineering, road engineering, municipal engineering, landscape engineering, environmental pollution prevention, and conservation of historical and cultural relics, among others. The organization has embarked on thousands of projects in China, Africa, and South America that include, among many, Shanghai Tower, Fangfei Garden of the Diaoyutai State Guest House, Table Tennis Gymnasium of the 2008 Olympic Games, African Union Conference Center, New Jinggangshan Revolution Museum, Shanghai Xintiandi, Theme Pavilion of the 2010 Shanghai Expo, Shanghai International Tourist Resort, Shanghai Natural History Museum, Shanghai Symphony Orchestra Concert Hall, China Corporate United Pavilion of Expo 2015 Milan, Havana Hotel of Cuba, Saikang Di Stadium of the Republic of Ghana, the National Arts Center of the Republic of Trinidad and Tobago, Sutong Yangtze River Highway Bridge, and Shanghai A5 (Jiading-Jinshan) Expressway Project.

Shanghai Tower
(Cooperative Design,
in partnership with
Gensler, Cosentini, and
Thornton Tomasetti)

Museum of Art Pudong
(Cooperative Design,
in partnership with
Ateliers Jean Nouvel)

Xi'an International Convention and Exhibition Center (Cooperative Design, in partnership with gmp and WES)

TJAD employs more than five thousand outstanding architectural design and engineering personnel to provide top engineering consulting services for our clients, and we have been working hard to promote urban development, so that we may build a better life for citizens through our many professional practices.

We firmly believe that it is the trust that our clients have in us that gives TJAD opportunities to grow. As part of the society and industry, we strive to continue to channel unremitting efforts toward industry development and social progress, just like we have been doing the past sixty-four years.

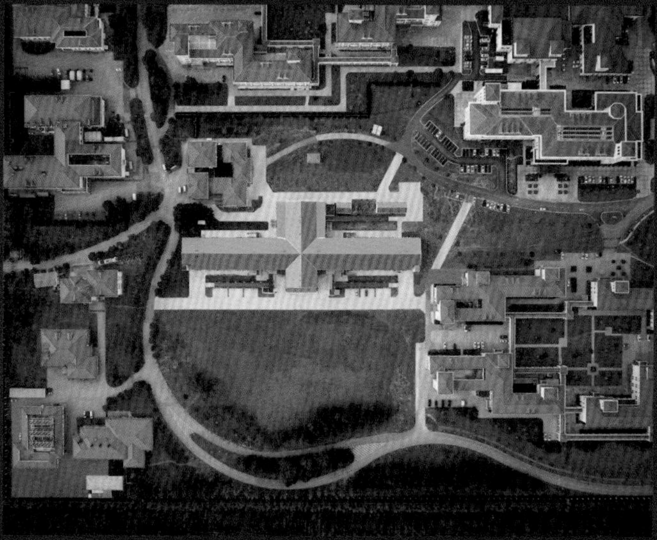

Contingency and Temporary Medical Building of Shanghai Public Health Clinical Center

Shangyin Opera House (Cooperative Design, in partnership with Christian de Portzamparc, Xu-Acoustique, and Theater Projects Consultants)